A FAMILY REMEMBERS

A FAMILY REMEMBERS

How to create a family memoir using video and tape recorders

Paul McLaughlin

Self-Counsel Press
(a division of)
International Self-Counsel Press Ltd.
Canada U.S.A.

Printed in Canada

First edition: October, 1993

Canadian Cataloguing in Publication Data

McLaughlin, Paul, 1950-
    A family remembers

    (Self-counsel series)
    ISBN 0-88908-293-6

    1. Genealogy.   2. Oral biography.   3. Video recordings — Production and direction.   4. Magnetic recorders and recording.   5. Interviewing.
I. Title. II. Series.
CS21.M235   1993   929'.2'028   C93-091780-4

Cover photography by Gary Ritchie Photography, Vancouver, B.C.

Excerpts from Peter Hitchcock's Videography: The Guide to Making Videos *are reprinted, with permission, by Peter Hitchcock Productions (Toronto).*

Self-Counsel Press
(*a division of*)
International Self-Counsel Press Ltd.

1481 Charlotte Road	1704 N. State Street
North Vancouver, British Columbia	Bellingham, Washington
V7J 1H1	98225

To Xenia, for memories past, present, and future.

CONTENTS

ACKNOWLEDGMENTS

My first and deepest appreciation must go to my wife, Xenia Splawinski, for her always valuable and insightful suggestions on how to improve both the book and my often frenzied state of mind. And to my father, Jim McLaughlin, for graciously answering my questions during the taping of my initial video memoir.

Sincere thanks to Ruth Wilson, my excellent and considerate editor at Self-Counsel Press, for her far-ranging help and support.

Special thanks also to the many people who granted me interviews, especially those who answered my letters to the editor asking to hear from anyone who had made a taped memoir.

Finally, many words of gratitude to the members of my writing group — Lawrence Hill, Karen Levenson, Kim Moritsugu, Oakland Ross, Ron Ruskin, Mark Sabourin, Bert Simpson, and Christine Slater — for their ongoing encouragement and critical response.

1
A PERSONAL INTRODUCTION

Memory is history recorded in our brain, memory is a painter, it paints pictures of the past and of the day.

Grandma Moses

This book was inspired by a birth and a death. The birth was of my first child, Arianna, in early 1987; the death was of my mother more than 15 years before. Until Arianna's arrival, I don't remember ever thinking that I didn't have any film or tape recordings of my mother. Nor many photographs, for that matter. My parents grew up poor in Scotland and a camera was a luxury they could ill afford. By the time they could, some years following our immigration to Canada, anything of the *paparazzi* that might have been in them was long since repressed. Photographs were taken occasionally, but not as a matter of course. Like most people, they never thought to tape record their voice or their children's, and a movie camera seemed something far beyond their reach and capability. As a result, there is little audiovisual record of my immediate and extended family.

I was oblivious to this absence until Arianna's birth, when the emergence of a new generation connected me to the previous ones in a way that had never happened before. I suddenly realized my daughter would never know my mother beyond a scattering of poorly taken photographs and the stories told by me and the few others still around who knew her well. If only — those famous two words — we had a tape or movie, something more "alive," so to speak,

1

than the distant shots of her captured over the years by our inexpensive Instamatic. How sad, I thought, to have had the simple technology within our grasp and not employed it.

My sadness was for myself, too. There was a great deal about my mother I didn't know — and will never know — and at the time of her death in 1971, when I was 20, much was unresolved between us. In the years since, I've experienced many feelings about her, including deeply painful ones, but most of all I've become curious to know more about this complex and troubled person.

A tape recording or a home movie would hardly provide all the answers I'm after, but they would likely give me a few. I would give much to hear her voice, look in her face, watch how she held and moved her body, listen to her laugh, see her at play with our family. Apart from the enjoyment of reliving such moments, there would be insights too, I'm sure.

When my father came to visit his granddaughter in 1987, at a vibrant and healthy age 74, I decided to sit him down in front of a video camera and talk to him about his life. I didn't have anything as formal as a memoir in mind at the time, just an urgent sense to create some kind of "living portrait," as I described it when he arrived. "I want this for Arianna, for any future children I might have, and for me," I said.

The taping took place in my living room and lasted about 90 minutes. At the beginning, I asked questions while I operated the camera, which was mounted on a tripod. Then Xenia, my wife, took over the camera and I sat on the couch beside my father and continued our discussion. It was nothing fancy from a technical standpoint, for neither Xenia nor I were video experts, but neither was it a disaster. The content, however, was all I had hoped for. Not only did I have my father telling familiar and valued stories in his broad Glaswegian accent, I learned a few things too.

My father, Jim McLaughlin, was born in a small town just outside Glasgow called Milngavie. He came from a large, poor Catholic family of eight children, whose poverty was worsened by the death of his father when Jim was still in the womb. My father often refers to himself as a "posthumous baby" as a way of describing someone whose father dies before he's born.

I never knew most of my father's family except for two of his sisters, for my grandmother and the other siblings were dead or, in the case of my uncle Tommy, had disappeared, before I was old enough to remember them. I wasn't aware, until the video, that there had been two other children. "My father was buried beside the twins who had died in infancy," my father said, recounting information he had been told as a child. "[Tommy said there were] two little boxes in the grave, like violin cases."

Nor did I realize the extent of his family's poverty. I had known they were poor, but until the video I didn't appreciate the degree. "There were eleven of us in a house that had two rooms and a kitchen," my father said. That number included his mother, eight children, an uncle, and — unbelievable as it seems — a lodger. "I have memories of seven of us sleeping this way in bed," he said, interlocking fingers from both hands to show how some heads were at one end of the bed, some heads at the other.

I prompted him to talk about his soccer prowess, because he had been the star center forward with Milngavie Juniors, which won the Scottish Junior Championship in 1934. As national victors, the team's picture was on cigarette cards. I also knew he'd suffered a terrible bicycle accident around the same time but, until the taping in 1987, I didn't understand the long-term affect it had on his life.

"When I was 19 and at the top of my soccer career, I should have been a great hero locally and all the girls should have been after me, shouldn't they have," he said. "Like hell they did — because I had an accident and lost all my teeth. I was cycling down a hill and went over the handlebar and landed on my mouth. And here I was with a big horrible mouth full of nothing. Well, girls shunned me. I had about four years without teeth because in those days you didn't get false teeth as fast as you get them now. I kept away from a lot of social events because of that. I was very sensitive...it made me more of a loner. But also I did love the hills and the mountains and cycling and mountaineering. So that's how I enjoyed myself until perhaps 27. I rarely dated girls."

That story told me a lot about my father, such as why he hadn't married until age 34, which was late in those days, particularly for a handsome and popular Catholic. I gained a new and deeper understanding of his personality, which is a strong mix of extroversion and shyness, life-of-the-party and loner. As I am very much like him, as all children are influenced and shaped to varying degrees by the nature and experiences of their parents, the tape also held clues about myself. Watching it a few days later, chuckling at familiar anecdotes I'd heard (and often begged not to hear) so many times before, savoring the mundane and occasionally poignant memories he spun from my questions, I knew something very special had been created.

A few days later, driving in my car, I experienced an epiphany — a moment of clarity and inspiration. I had recently published a book on journalistic interviewing, which is one of my passions. Why not offer my skills as an interviewer to help people produce memoirs of their parents, grandparents, or anyone else they're close to? Thus was born the company Video Recorded Memories, one of my best creative ideas and one of my worst business ventures.

The media loved the idea and gave me a lot of free publicity. The public loved the idea and gave me a lot of calls — but few contracts. To produce the memoirs to the standard

I wanted, I had to charge more than it turned out people were willing to pay. My decision to quietly close down the company in late 1988 came not long after spending several hours planning a memoir in the company of a woman and her aging parents. As we made final preparations for the taping, I asked the woman for my usual 50% retainer. I had assumed she knew the price, but she didn't. Upon hearing it she became visibly upset. "Oh my," she said. "If I pay you, then I can't afford to go south this winter, and I've been looking forward to the trip for ages. I know I'll probably regret this decision for the rest of my life, but...." I'd heard a variation of that response many times before, but this was the proverbial last "but." Although I had done many interesting and enjoyable memoirs along the way, I felt it was time to put a good idea to rest.

Along with the "buts" was another compelling argument for tucking Video Recorded Memories into bed for a long, if not permanent, sleep. Camcorder sales were booming as prices dropped and the equipment became easier to use. Why should people pay me, I conceded, to do something they could do themselves? They had the equipment, all some of them lacked was the know-how. Epiphany #2 flashed across my mental screen: I should write a book.

Other projects consumed my time over the next few years but I never lost interest and enthusiasm for the concept. In the back of my mind I knew one day I would commit to paper my ideas and suggestions about how video and audio memoirs can be made. That time is now; and I've provided this brief history so you'll know my experience and credentials for writing this book.

This is also the time to assure any of you concerned who might think this is too technical a book. What follows is not a convoluted manual or a crash course on the latest whizbang digital effects. It is first and foremost a guide for people with average consumer knowledge of the technical aspects of video and audio. I've tried to avoid technical jargon, keeping the discussions on lighting, sound, etc. to a level that anyone who can change a light bulb can understand. There is one chapter devoted to more advanced production techniques, but those of you with no interest in them can skip it without losing anything necessary to accomplish your goal.

In the following chapters I explore the various shapes and forms that memoirs can take. Please be assured, however, that these are only suggestions and guidelines. The last thing I want is for you to feel intimidated or restricted.

I wish you well with your endeavors in producing family memoirs. Whether the final product is simply a conversation with someone you love or an intricate documentary of your family history, you will never regret the time and effort devoted to its creation.

2
MEMOIRS ARE WHAT YOU MAKE THEM

*To forget one's ancestors is to be a brook without
a source, a tree without a root.*

Chinese proverb

At some point in life, usually as we approach the denouement of our time on earth, many of us consider writing our memoirs or family history. But a scarce few of us ever do, and for good reason. Writing a book is an onerous undertaking at best, and too overwhelming for all but a small number to accomplish. As author Gene Fowler once put it, "Writing is easy; all you do is sit staring at a blank sheet of paper until the drops of blood form on your forehead." But there is little bloodshed when creating a taped memoir — unless you drop the equipment on your foot. A memoir is well within the reach of anyone who can follow a simple set of technical and production guidelines such as this book provides.

Within our homes (or as close as the nearest rental outlet) is equipment that allows us to do what all but the most recent generations in history could only dream of: produce high-quality recordings of ourselves and others. Typically, camcorders are brought out at birthdays, weddings, family holidays and other significant events. Tape recorders are used less often to tape family events, more to send taped messages to distant relatives and friends.

Curiously, this equipment is rarely used to *create* material. Rather, it's employed almost journalistically, to record events that are happening whether the camcorder or tape recorder is there or not. Many people have said to me, "I never thought of using my camcorder to ask granny about her life. How could I not have considered that?" I don't know the answer for sure, but I'll venture three possible reasons.

One is the influence of advertising. You videotaped the family birthday party because that's what advertising has led you to understand a camcorder is for. It's not surprising people use camcorders to capture the same events they traditionally photograph. A lifetime's inundation of Kodak commercials do have their effect. If camcorder manufacturers promoted their product as the perfect means of producing family memoirs, you can bet your pension plan that family memoir production would skyrocket.

The second reason is more complex. The most common (although by no means the only) taped memoir involves an intimate conversation between an adult and someone elderly, typically a parent or grandparent. To propose such a conversation requires the discussion or, at least, the implied discussion, of that elderly person's mortality, and, ultimately, of your own. Ours is not a society that makes such a dialogue easy or appealing to most people. "I wouldn't want my parents to feel I'm thinking they're about to die," a friend of mine said, explaining why he wouldn't be comfortable asking them to tape a memoir. "I know it would make them uneasy."

Perhaps my friend was right in the context of his family, but my sense is that it's more often the younger person who is uncomfortable with the subject of death than the older. "Philosophically, I think most older people, myself included, are quite prepared to die," says 67-year-old Barry Broadfoot, the author of nine books of oral histories, including *Ten Lost Years*, in which he chronicled the stories of ordinary Canadians during the Depression. "'Death for most of us will come as an old friend' as King George the Fifth said." But for most younger people, and by that I especially mean the middle-aged, death is more like an unfriendly skeleton in the closet, rarely talked about and only then in hushed and embarrassed tones.

8

There is also a sentiment shared by many within our society that reminiscence is a negative pursuit. "One of the more persistent images of old age fuses, or rather confuses, the age-old activity of reminiscence with hopelessness, denial of death, turning away from present realities, loss of memory, and intellectual deterioration," writes Marc Kaminsky in *The Uses of Reminiscence: A Discussion of the Formative Literature:*

> In the *Rhetoric,* Aristotle wrote of old people that 'They live by memory rather than by hope, for what is left to them of life is but little compared to the long past. This, again, is the cause of their loquacity. They are continually talking of the past, because they enjoy remembering.' This passage is less remarkable in its error than in its perspicacity. The conviction that old age is necessarily hopeless because of its close proximity to death is still with us, and still distorts our perception of old people. Of great interest is Aristotle's recognition of the value of reminiscence: it is not only a source of pleasure, but it helps old people cope with their knowledge of the imminence of death.

The third reason is another potential discouragement. Relationships between parents and children are often strained and there can be fear, anger or awkwardness about asking someone to talk about sensitive or unresolved issues. Although Broadfoot has taped oral histories with literally thousands of people, he confides that he could never interview his own mother:

> There's a lot of [unresolved issues] in our family, and my mother is just not the kind of person who would do it [a taping]. Which is too bad because she's 95 and one of the true Canadian pioneers. The youngest of 12, all born on a rug on the kitchen floor with my

grandfather acting as a midwife. She's got a million stories to tell but I don't do her because I wouldn't feel comfortable. I'll just give you one example. She lives in Winnipeg and three years ago we were driving down the original Main Street. We pass City Hall, and she just casually says, "You know, your grandfather could have bought that land for $2 an acre...but instead he went 20 miles out into the bush and hacked out a farm." It would be great to have stories like that on tape.

But for others, like Joyce Stephenson of Oakville, Ontario, doing a memoir with a parent was a comfortable and mutually beneficial experience. Stephenson taped numerous conversations in the late 1980s with her mother, who was born in 1897. "She was very open and we had always been close," says Stephenson. "She was like an open book herself, she could never hold back things and be secretive. I was particularly interested in certain problems in the family. Like why so and so felt this way about so and so. We really analyzed a lot of characteristics of the various members of the family."

The decision to propose a family memoir should not be taken without consideration of the potential emotional effects it might have on everyone involved and on their relationship with each other. Therefore, it's essential to plan and present the idea properly (see chapter 3).

WHO SHOULD MAKE MEMOIRS?

Everyone and anyone, no matter what age. Although this book tends to include examples of memoirs in which an elderly person is the subject of a memoir rather than the actual creator of it, it is not meant to suggest the very young or old shouldn't be making memoirs too.

"I get a great deal of satisfaction out of what I'm doing," says Morris Silbert, who at age 80 has taped about 40 family memoirs. "It has given me a goal in life, and one of the problems with retirement is that people who don't have a goal can feel useless."

WHAT IS A VIDEO OR AUDIO MEMOIR?

"In the past, families kept in touch by writing letters — letters which were often carefully stored in basements or attics for future generations," write authors Ellen Robinson Epstein and Rona Mendelsohn in *Record and Remember: Tracing Your Roots Through Oral History.* "Letters were a family link. Today we pick up the phone when we want to learn the latest family news. Phone calls leave no traces of daily life to pass on. We need to have concrete objects such as letters to preserve our past. However, letter-writing is too tedious for many people. The tape [and video] recording of memories is the twentieth century answer to written memoirs."

As I suggested in the Introduction, there's no rigid definition of these twentieth century memoirs, as far as I'm concerned. Nor should there be. There are certain shapes and forms they can take but those depend solely on you.

Before outlining some of those basic structures, I think it's helpful to examine what distinguishes a taped memoir from the contemporaneous recording of a birthday party, wedding, or some other typical family event.

The difference for me is that a taped memoir is the deliberate, planned use of a camcorder or tape recorder to elicit and preserve life stories that otherwise might be lost forever upon the death of the storyteller. The stories can encompass just about any aspect of a one's personal, family, or cultural history — the range of possibilities is endless. There is a purpose in mind, and that purpose is to create a family archive for present and future generations, containing the experiences, passions, triumphs, failures, sorrows, daily routines and anything else deemed significant in day-to-day life. In comparison, the contemporaneous recording of family events, such as birthdays and weddings, rarely includes such material. They are more like moving snapshots of important moments as they happen, equally valuable but rarely introspective or retrospective.

I also want to re-emphasize that you should not be intimidated into thinking your memoir has to be some slick production made to the standards of professional TV or radio. You may very well accomplish such a memoir, but to my thinking it doesn't matter whether it's amateurish, has technical mistakes or, to an outsider, seems dull and unstructured. Obviously it's better to produce a lively, structured tape; and this book is presented to help you accomplish that goal. But the bottom line for me is that the preservation of stories far surpasses the need to entertain an audience.

Make the memoirs first and foremost for yourself. If you don't feel competent or interested in editing the finished product, don't worry about it. Let future generations package and hone the material if they want to. Imagine it this way. What if we had taped memoirs from 200 years ago? From 500 or 1,000 years ago? What value would we place on those? Would we immediately run out and edit them down to a 60-minute, fast-paced package? I find it interesting that when friends hear me explain the memoir concept one of their first reactions is to predict the tapes will be too long and boring. Interestingly, most choose 60 minutes as the prescribed length, coincidentally the same length of the average TV show. I agree that a long, boring tape is...well, long and boring. But I'd give my eye teeth for some long and boring tapes of my mother and grandparents.

THE MOST BASIC STRUCTURE

It can't get any easier than this: prepare what you want to talk about, sit the storyteller in a comfortable chair, turn on a camcorder or tape recorder, have a relaxed conversation, make some copies of the unedited tape and, voila, instant heirloom.

If it's a video memoir, focus the camera on the teller the entire time. Decide whether you're going to operate the camera yourself or have someone else do it for you (see chapter 10).

The above also applies to situations where you interview more than one person at the same time, such as both your parents or both a grandmother and grandfather.

VARIATION ON THE BASIC THEME

Now it's time to explore some of the various guises a memoir can take — beyond the most basic structure. The list of suggestions that follow is by no means definitive. I'm sure you will come up with many other variations.

Serial conversations

Record a series of unedited conversations with the subject of the memoir. Typically, each conversation will concentrate on one specific topic or time period. A word of caution, though. Arranging and following through with a series of interviews requires a considerable commitment on both your part and that of the teller. It's easy for the project to become delayed or abandoned due to dwindling energy or enthusiasm. To avoid this happening, make a firm interview schedule in advance and stick to it.

Edited conversations

After recording the conversation(s), edit the tape slightly to take out the rambling, repetitious, and any other unneeded parts. If you don't know how to edit (see chapter 11), get someone else to do it for you.

You edit this type of memoir with the intent to retain as much of the original interview(s) as possible while eliminating material that wouldn't be missed.

Highly produced conversations

Highly produced conversations involve production techniques that give the conversation a more polished look. In addition to editing unwanted material, you might add music, still photographs (for video memoirs), sound effects (for audio memoirs), and other elements (see chapter 12) to make the finished product more entertaining, like a full-length TV, radio, or film interview.

Documentary

This usually involves the telling of a grander theme, such as your family history, by editing comments from several interviewees into a highly produced tape or series of tapes. It is often narrated, fast-paced, and features shorter "clips" (sections of an interview) rather than long, unedited comments from one or more speaker.

Biography

Similar in form to the documentary, the biography concentrates not on a family history but on the story of one individual. Typically, it features selected comments by the subject of the biography (if available) and people who knew him or her.

Autobiography

Almost like a journal, an autobiography can be as straightforward as you talking directly to a camcorder or tape recorder in either a well-planned or spontaneous delivery. Likewise, it can remain "raw" (unedited) or can be highly produced.

BEWARE HAGIOGRAPHY

The word hagiography (meaning the biography of saints) is used disparagingly to define uncritical stories that idealize and sanitize the life of the person being portrayed. All the blemishes are removed or ignored while the good points are trumpeted to the high heavens. As a result, the subject is elevated to the status of saint.

In *Writing the Family Narrative*, Lawrence Gouldrup warns against hagiography:

> Perhaps the pitfall that claims most beginners is the almost universal human drive to protect those closest and dearest to them. Basically, it is the problem of what we should or should not tell about ourselves or our families. Many of us feel obligated to spare the readers the ignominy of our ancestors. I can offer no easy solution but [to say that] no one believes a "bowdlerized" or idealized version of someone's life. There are too many family histories that deal only with someone's goodness, courage, determination, or faith in God. On the other hand, many writers feel that no story is interesting unless it is filled with the shocking and the seamy. Perhaps the best approach is a compromise somewhere between the idealized and the sensational.

Toronto psychiatrist (and novelist) Dr. Ron Ruskin endorses Gouldrup's advice. "I feel the interest in a story is based on the character *not being* a saint," says Ruskin. "I think that [hagiography] takes away from a person's humanity. But I guess it comes down to the question of purpose of the memoir: Is it to get at the truth or to paint a pretty picture?"

3
PLANNING MAKES BETTER
(NOTHING'S PERFECT)

It takes me about three weeks to write a good impromptu speech.

Mark Twain

Steven Spielberg does it. Norman Jewison does it. Penny Marshall does it too. Planning, that is, and if movie directors consider it one of the most critical building blocks of a successful production, why shouldn't you?

There's obviously no rule forbidding you from turning on the camera or tape recorder and firing away without any foresight. It's possible you'll end up with a valuable and worthwhile result. From my experience, however, more often than not you will fall short of what could have been achieved. Mary Casey of Dartmouth, Nova Scotia, experienced that first hand. "We videotaped my grandmother at her nursing home about 2 years before her death, when she was 96," she says. "After watching it, I realized there was so much more I could have asked her. I should have been more prepared."

The two hardest parts of any creative project are getting started — taking that first step beyond the idea of doing something to actually beginning the work in a meaningful way — and seeing the project through to completion. Many a brilliant flash of inspiration never gets beyond the fantasizing stage.

One way to overcome procrastination and lack of follow-through is to develop a clear and simple plan you can realistically accomplish. Setting realistic goals is especially

16

important. Although I encourage you to aim high creatively, I also caution against designing a project so grandiose and complicated you'll never be able to achieve it. Better to have a humble tape completed and on the shelf than a major motion picture that plays only in your mind.

While formulating a plan is no guarantee you'll put it in action, it's my experience that it greatly increases the chance of success. That's because the planning process forces you to think out what you intend to do (especially if you write it down) and how you're going to accomplish it. It necessitates that you clarify and organize your goals. At the same time, keep in mind that, once established, your plan should not be cast in stone, for it will likely evolve as you go along.

Some amateurs believe planning is only required for professional works, but it's actually the opposite. The less you know, the more important planning becomes. "It helps to have some kind of plan, especially if you don't have much experience with this kind of thing," Studs Terkel advises during a telephone interview from the Chicago radio station where he works. The legendary oral historian, whose books such as *Hard Times* and *American Dreams* resonate with the stories of "the non-celebrated," as he puts it, suggests you "take some time figurin' out what you're gonna do."

How much "figurin'" is up to you, but I suggest you keep the following in mind:

- Spend enough time planning until you're clear about what you want to accomplish, how you're going to accomplish it, what you need to do in advance to ensure the plan succeeds, and how ambitious your project is going to be.

- Be aware you can plan a project to death. Procrastination often adopts the guise of planning and research. Some people spend all their time planning but never actually get down to work.

THE FIRST STEP

"The first step is deciding on the focus of your family video," says Katherine Stanton in her production *Make A Family Video Album*. "What's the purpose...the game plan?"

For example, it makes a considerable difference whether you intend to focus on the entire life of your grandmother or just one particular period, such as her childhood, the Depression years or the war years. If you're producing a family memoir, what time period will you cover, how many sides of the family, what particular issues or events (such as the family business, immigrating to North America, etc.)?

One way to help determine the focus is to imagine the finished tape in your mind. If you could wave a magic wand to make the final product appear, where would it start, what stories would it tell, how would it end? Another is to assemble a group of people for a production meeting where you brainstorm what you want to accomplish.

GUEST LIST

Identify who you want to interview for the memoir. Often it's just one person — the subject of the memoir — but don't make that decision without considering whether it might be better to include others. If you decide to have several speakers — and there's a selection process involved — choose people who you know to be lively and confident conversationalists (if possible).

As noted previously, being interviewed can be too intimidating or uncomfortable for some people to achieve any comfort level. I certainly encourage you to record interviews with those who are not great speakers, but I also advise you not to put someone through an hour or so of hell (plus all the worry leading up to it) if the end result is a tape that's too painful to watch or listen to. If a person is terrified of being recorded, you might have to abandon your project rather than try to force an unworkable situation, especially with someone elderly and perhaps emotionally vulnerable.

WHAT FORM WILL IT TAKE?

As discussed in chapter 2, you should decide the structure and production level of the memoir in advance (is it one, long unedited interview, a documentary, etc.?). That decision will have a considerable impact on your plan and how you enact it.

If, for example, you hope to produce a tape that will be interesting and entertaining for family members, one that has a professional look, you'll need to plan extensively. On the other hand, if your goal is to simply have an unedited interview for your own private purpose, your planning requirements will be reduced considerably.

HOW LONG IS THE FINISHED PRODUCT?

A producer shooting a thirty-minute film has different planning needs than a producer shooting three hour-long segments. The biggest difference is that you need a lot more material for three hours than for thirty minutes.

If your mind's eye envisages a two-hour unedited reminiscence by one person, ask yourself if that person has two hours worth of stories to tell. Two hours is a long time for a shy or taciturn person, for example, to speak. If you're making the tape for distribution within your family, be forewarned that few speakers can hold an audience's attention for two hours of non-stop talking, no matter how engaging they seem to you.

For a family history, determine in advance if there are enough people living who can provide the information you want to include and, if not, if you have access to other sources (through research) that can be conveyed in a taped memoir.

LOCATION

The standard location is in the subject's home, especially if you're interviewing someone whose age or health eliminates any other choice. Mobility aside, the home is usually the preferred location because of the memories it can evoke. "If I had done a video of my granny, I would have done it in her apartment because everything in it was a special object to her," says Daphne Ballon, a producer for Toronto's prestigious Atlantis Films. "I would have had her after dinner with a scotch, and I know she would have told a million stories. It would have been a combination of the objects in the room, the shape of the apartment, the photos on the wall. I would have cut that in with video from my sister's wedding. Granny went up and did a dirty limerick in front of the whole wedding. It was very funny. She had a bad memory but she never forgot a dirty limerick."

However, if your memoir subject is mobile, it's worth questioning whether there's a more suitable location, especially one with an interesting visual or sound backdrop. "It would be great to take someone walking around a town, looking at all the old landmarks, whether they're still there or not," suggests filmmaker and producer David Stringer, the host of TV Ontario's eight-part series "Successful Home Video." "They tend to relax while they're doing that as well, because they're not so aware of the camera."

Here are some other location examples, to stimulate your imagination:

- For a segment on wartime memories, an interview could be conducted at a war museum or memorial (keeping in mind that it might also be too painful an association for the interviewee and, therefore, must be discussed and agreed to in advance).

- A person who loves gardening could be interviewed in the garden or while tending to indoor plants.

- A tour of the family farm (if it's not in the family's possession, the owner might grant permission to visit if the purpose is clearly explained) could enhance an interview with parents/grandparents who lived there most of their life.

It's important to consider location for tape-recorded interviews as well as video ones. In addition to the potential stimulation evoked by the surroundings, the tape will also contain the sounds of the location, such as birds, wind, a running stream, machinery, children laughing, cars, whatever the ear can hear.

PROPS

"I plunked the strings of a spinet that had been in the family for 150 years," says Greg Stone in his article "History in the (Video) Making," published in *Videomaker* magazine. "This physical object gave me the opportunity to talk about the people who had originally purchased and used it. An old family Bible provided the focal point for a conversation with my brother in yet another segment."

As with locations, props can trigger memories and associations, as well as serving to enliven the visual (and sound) qualities of a memoir. The most obvious props are photographs and family albums. Others include —

- Letters (which can be read as part of the memoir).

- Paintings (especially if painted by the subject or someone close to the him or her).

- Musical instruments (an interview could be conducted at the family piano, for example, which could lead to an impromptu or planned performance).

- War medals, ration books, trophies, newspaper clippings, certificates, old baseball gloves, toys, any other memorabilia.

SELLING THE PROJECT

Your project can be completely scuttled if you don't elicit cooperation from the people you need to interview. As journalists know only too well, how you propose or "sell" an idea can have great bearing on whether it goes ahead. Consequently, you don't want to make a wrong move, one that may be irreversible, when asking the subject of your memoir and/or other interviewees to participate. See chapter 6 for more detailed information.

RESEARCH

Research is conducted for two primary reasons: to inspire interesting and pertinent questions and to help you relax during the interview. The first benefit seems self-explanatory, but how does research accomplish the latter? If you know your subject, feel secure about the quality (and quantity) of your questions, you will likely feel more confident. As a result, your listening and intuitive skills will be freed up to work at their optimum level. A nervous and unprepared questioner is too busy panicking and scanning his or her brain for the next question to function well on these more subtle — but just as important — aspects of communication.

You might forego research if you know enough about the people you're interviewing, and the topics and time periods you intend to discuss. If that's not the case, your research might include the following steps.

Books, films, and other information about the time periods

It's helpful to be well acquainted with the history and culture of the various pivotal periods in your subject's life. A valuable and interesting way to gain insight is through books and films that depict the times accurately. These can range from historical accounts to specialty books or documentaries on fashion, music, inventions, architecture and countless other topics. The best source is the library followed by secondhand book stores and video rental outlets.

Newspaper stories

This is my favorite research source. Newspapers contain enormous amounts of information, both "big picture" and "small detail." They reveal the stories, issues, debates, values, and countless other essential elements of a country and/or community, and they provide meaningful tidbits such as the price of goods, popular music, hit films, fads, etc.

Most past editions of local newspapers are available on microfilm in your library. In large cities, certain libraries will carry past editions of the major papers from other cities and countries as well.

When searching through old newspapers, keep a sharp lookout for articles about, or of interest to, your subject. One idea is to read what happened on the day the subject (or yourself, for an autobiographical memoir) was born. In most libraries you can make photocopies off the microfilm. These make wonderful conversation starters during an interview. They can also be recorded with your camcorder and edited into a video memoir or read as part of a tape recorded one.

Local history association

Most communities have an historical society. Not only will the society have books, newspaper articles, documents and other reading/broadcast materials about your community, the members will either have direct knowledge about local history, lore, and characters or can put you in touch with someone who does.

Other people

One of the best and most bountiful sources of information is conversation with other people. There are divergent views on whether you should talk with the subject of your interview beforehand. One school of thought argues against, citing that the person will shy away from repeating stories during the actual taping, frame an answer with "as I told you before" and other potential negative side effects of having done a dry run. The opposite viewpoint notes the wealth of information garnered about the interviewee — what questions work best, foreknowledge of anecdotes that sizzle or fizzle, insight to the interviewee's character, voice quality, physical limitations, sensitive areas, etc.

I agree with both sides. A pre-interview, as journalists call it, always yields invaluable material. But if it happens too close to the time of the actual taping, some of the fallout noted above can occur. Possible solutions: do the pre-interview well in advance of the taping date, or have it done by someone other than the interviewer.

Another option is to talk beforehand with someone who knows a lot about the storyteller. This often provides information not available or forthcoming from the teller, such as tips on what questions to ask or stories to draw out; areas to probe or to avoid; health, energy, temperament of the teller; and other useful details that otherwise you wouldn't have known.

The range of people to talk with is endless. In addition to family members (search out the ones keen on family history), you could contact friends, business associates and anyone who knows (or knew) your subject well. If your research demands an understanding of topics beyond the family history — for example, certain military activities during World War II — your preparation for the interview might include conversations with military history experts who have no personal connection to the teller. Don't be afraid to phone experts in the government, universities, or anywhere else you can find them. Most are only too eager to talk about their area of expertise.

Genealogical information

A family memoir is not a family tree, but it's possible the project, or your research requirements, will lead you to begin or enhance your knowledge of who's who in your family background.

Two resources for acquiring genealogical information, among many available, are the following:

(a) The Genealogical Department of the Church of Jesus Christ of Latter-Day Saints. The Church's library in Salt Lake City, Utah, is the world's largest storehouse of genealogical records. Its 1,800,000 reels of micro-filmed records, as of 1993, is equivalent to 6 million 300-page bound volumes. The Church operates more than 1,800 Family History Centers in 55 countries, with approximately 80 branches in Canada.

(b) The Genealogical Research Library, 80 Gerrard Street East, Suite #18-D, Toronto, Canada M5B 2J1. For a fee, GRL offers a "research case" service, in which it assigns a professional genealogist to trace your family tree; or a "specific search" method, in which it responds to your specific research question(s).

DON'T (YOU CAN'T) TELL THE WHOLE STORY!

A taped memoir is not a book with endless pages available. It's not possible to get down every little detail in a one-hour or longer tape. Get a video biography from the library or your local video store to see what can be accomplished in 60 to 120 minutes. Even if you plan to produce a series of interviews with the memoir subject, each tape can only cover so much ground.

If you accept the limitations of the medium beforehand, you'll set more realistic goals for the actual interviews and any production techniques you plan to employ.

4
INVOKING MEMORIES

I remember my father said to me something about memory. He said, "I thought I could recall my childhood when we first came to Buenos Aires, but now I know that I can't. Every time I recall something I'm not really recalling it really, I'm recalling the last time I recalled it, I'm recalling my last memory of it."

Jorge Louis Borges

My mother, sister and I left Scotland to join my father in Canada — he had gone over several months earlier to find a job — on August 8, 1957, my seventh birthday. The timing of our departure has always seemed significant to me, as if the first part of my life had come to a complete close, and the next was starting fresh. I remember little of the hurly-burly days around our leaving, but a few images remain clear and vibrant. One was riding in a car for the first time, from Milngavie to the harbor at Greenock from where we sailed. I don't recall the car in detail, but I have impressions of a black vehicle shining in the sun, of me and my sister small and obedient on the plush back seat. Aboard the Fairsea, a Greek ocean liner with an Italian crew (I had forgotten the name, but my sister, Hilary, remembered), nothing is more firmly etched in my memory than the taste of my first Coca-Cola, and how I couldn't get enough of those small brown bottles. It's never tasted nearly as good since. I also remember hitting my sister, who was a year-and-a-half older, on the head with a toy gun; trying to play shuffleboard on deck; scanning the horizon longingly for icebergs; and eating lumpy cream of mushroom soup at dinner.

We docked in Quebec City on August 15 and there set foot on Canadian soil for the first time. There were several hours before our train to Hamilton, where my father, like many Scots before him, had gravitated to find work in the steel mills. To pass the time, my mother hailed a taxi and asked the driver to take us for a tour. He was a kind old man and drove us to all the sights, including the historic Plains of Abraham. He insisted on buying an ice cream for Hilary and me and, if he charged my mother at all for that wonderful tour of old Quebec—I doubt she had any Canadian money— I know it was a fraction of what it should have cost.

Are my memories accurate? I assume that most are true to what occurred, but some may also be faulty, embellished, or acquired from accounts told by my mother or sister over the years and incorporated as my own. I don't think it matters, at least not to me. These are the impressions I carry with me of that important time, and I treasure them dearly. Perhaps other recollections will arise as more time passes, but unless I'm given corroborating evidence — my sister's memory being the only possible source — I'll never know if something retrieved from my memory really happened or if it arose from my imagination because of some present need to perceive the past in a particular way.

Memory is exceptionally subjective and vulnerable to passing time. If your goal in talking with a relative is to secure unimpeachable recollections, I doubt you will achieve it. Some stories and details will be accurate, but others will have been polished over time, sanitized, distorted, invented, and remain otherwise unreliable from a purely historical point of view.

My goal in making a taped memoir is to capture what a person remembers, feels, and thinks and to preserve that subjective record in his or her own voice and image. I believe it's just as interesting — if not more so — to discover how

27

someone remembers and chooses to describe or explain that memory than it is to try and pin down some elusive "truth" about the past. Especially, if in doing so, the emotions of the present get cast aside as inconsequential. "In a now celebrated article, Dr. Robert Butler argued that reminiscence is really a form of life review undertaken in old age," writes Harry Moody in *Reminiscence and the Recovery of the Public World*. "Old people, approaching the limits of their life, retrieve memories of the past in order to work through unresolved conflicts — regret, grief, guilt, unfulfilled dreams. This working through of the memories of the past is indeed like the work of our dreams during sleep, and it fulfills a similar psychic function in maintaining our mental equilibrium in the face of losses, frustrations, and the accumulated anxieties of a lifetime."

If given a choice between a clear and accurate memory rather than a clouded or confabulated one, I naturally prefer the former. This chapter includes ideas to help you invoke memory and better understand the complexity of this fascinating dimension of the human mind.

FORGET YOUR PRECONCEPTIONS ABOUT MEMORY

Society tends to depict all old people as forgetful. It is a mistake to do so. While some elderly people might suffer a degree of memory impairment as a result of diseases such as anemia, blood-vessel disorders, hardening of the arteries, and goiter, others experience no noticeable decline. "Gerontologists say there's no positive proof that 'mental deficiency' comes at any certain age," writes David Lewis in *The Miracle of Instant Memory Power*, "except perhaps in extreme age."

Dr. Jane Dywan, an assistant professor of psychology at Brock University, is an expert on memory and aging (see interview with Dr. Dywan in chapter 5). She strongly cautions interviewers not to harbor preconceived notions about an elderly person's ability to recall. "The individual differences in older people are greater than at any other age group," she says.

Another stereotype is that elderly people can't remember mundane details from the present, such as where they put their glasses, but can vividly recall events from their childhood many decades past. "It's true that as some people grow older it gets harder and harder to learn new information, remember new names and numbers, the details of everyday life," says Dywan. "But again there are huge individual differences." That latter point was clearly brought home to Joyce Stephenson over a several-year period during which she interviewed her elderly mother about her life. Stephenson's mother, who was in her late eighties at the time, came to Oakville for visits from Saskatchewan. "Many times when she would come, she remembered something I'd told her the time before," says Stephenson. "I wouldn't remember it and I'd think, geez, how could she do that. She was very sharp."

In *The Miracle of Instant Memory Power*, David Lewis cites several research projects that refute society's assumptions about memory and aging. One was a study of factors such as judgment, perception, and memory power conducted by Dr. Ward Halstead, professor of psychology and director of medical psychology at the University of Chicago. "Beyond [age] 50," Lewis writes, "[Halstead] found deterioration was slightly greater, with most breakdowns taking place in the sixties and seventies. Significantly, the drop in mental deficiency was so slight that it made no appreciable difference in performance. 'The added experience,' [Halstead] said, 'more than overcame the slight loss of brain power in most cases.' His conclusion: the brain does not necessarily age as tissues of the body do."

Another study Lewis notes took place at Columbia University: "Dr. Irving Lodge found that students up to 70 and above could learn Russian and shorthand as easily as their younger classmates could."

I mention these professional opinions on memory and aging not as gospel truth — I'm not qualified on the subject — but as an inspiration and challenge to examine your own attitudes about elderly people and their degree of mental faculty before you embark on creating a memoir. In our western society, unlike many other cultures, old age is rarely valued as a new and exciting stage of life, the last great adventure on the inevitable and natural progression to death. Instead, it's more often cast as a time of decay rather than growth.

I'm a great believer that the attitude you bring to an interview can affect the outcome. It's not a law in which A=B, but I've seen enough evidence to know that the way you approach people can make a difference. Therefore, if you expect your elderly guest to be feeble-minded and doting, you might actually contribute to that result occurring. On the other hand, if you treat your guest with dignity and assume reasonable expectations, your chance of encountering such responses probably rises.

SETTING MEMORY GOALS

"Remembering," says Edmund Blair Bolles in *Remembering and Forgetting: An Inquiry into the Nature of Memory*, "is an act of imagination. For several thousand years people have believed that remembnering retrieves information stored somewhere in the mind...[that there's] a memory warehouse where the past lies preserved like childhood souvenirs in an attic." According to Bolles (and other memory experts), "memory is a living product of desire, attention, insight and consciousness." In other words, the more effort we put into remembering, the more we are likely to remember. "We have not appreciated memory's active nature," explains Bolles:

> Instead of saying so-and-so has a great memory, implying the same passive accomplishment of a person whose eyes are a beautiful shade of green, we come closer to the mark in saying so-and-so is a great rememberer.

Remembering well is like running well or playing well. It is not for the lazy and not for the fearful. The veil of paradox disappears, however, if we think of forgetfulness as a failure to create a memory instead of a failure to retrieve one. Forgetting is like striking out at the plate. We were not up to the occasion.

One means of activating the memory, according to David Lewis, is to provide motivation. "Generally speaking," he says, "the stronger the motive or reason for remembering, the more efficiently the memory functions." If you want to improve your own memory, or someone else's, he suggests finding reasons for remembering, or memory goals.

ENTHUSIASM: THE ULTIMATE MEMORY GOAL

Based on the theories of memory experts, it would seem crucial to plan your memoir in conjunction with the subject. Rather than surprising someone, as I did with my father, you'll likely elicit a greater number of vivid memories if you discuss the project in advance and, in doing so, gain the enthusiastic cooperation of the subject. Lewis says interest is a vital ingredient in involving the proper attitude for memory. Therefore, if the subject of the memoir feels excited about the project, an effective memory goal is established.

The responsibility for stoking that interest lies partly with you. "Nothing is so contagious as enthusiasm," wrote the English novelist Edward Bulwer-Lytton. "It moves stones, it charms brutes. Enthusiasm is the genius of sincerity, and truth accomplishes no victories without it." The victory, in your case, might be to inspire a reluctant, unsure, or nervous participant into becoming a willing partner, a creative collaborator in a project that has everlasting value. Conversely, if you don't project interest for the task you're proposing, don't be surprised if you're turned down or the final product falls below your expectations.

Once the subject has been won over, you can assist his or her memory by outlining specific areas you intend to cover during the taping. This will provide the person with the time and foreknowledge to start thinking back to the past.

PHOTOGRAPHS, CUE CARDS, AND OTHER REMINDERS

Memory begins with reminders, the most obvious of which are photographs, other memorabilia, and a familiar (and comfortable) setting, as discussed in chapter 3. Another is cue cards, an idea that came from social worker Paula David, who used them for two memoir projects at Toronto's Baycrest Geriatric Centre:

> I was working with a creative writing group who were writing their memoirs...and Global TV, as part of its coverage of Canada's 125th birthday [in 1992], wanted to interview some of them. Naturally the people were nervous. So I wrote the questions, about ten of them, that the interviewer wanted to ask, on bristol board, in big printing, as simply as possible, to help keep them on track...and be relaxed.

> I could see cue cards being used for memoirs with some people, particularly the very elderly or very nervous people, or people who have trouble staying on track. It could help keep them focused, keep them from rambling by reminding them of what the original question was.

WRITING DOWN MEMORIES

An unused memory, like an old machine, can rust and stop moving. One way to oil it back to peak form is through writing, particularly if the writing is done consistently over a period of times. In *At the Center of the Story*, Grace Worth, of the

National Council on Aging, recounts the benefits of writing down memories experienced by an oral history group she led in Cincinnati in 1980:

> Each person had a piece of yellow lined tablet paper and a pencil in front of him or her. I told them to begin by putting a small square in the middle of the paper and to mark it with an X. The square represented the home they lived in when they were about ten years old. The boundaries of the paper were the approximate boundaries of their home "territory," one edge being perhaps the big street over there that you weren't allowed to cross, or the creek you never walked beyond; another edge, the cemetery down the road a bit, or the street with the corner grocery store where you bought your milk and bread. Each one was to fill in within those boundaries a kind of map of the home-place, noting as many details as could be recalled — street or road names, names of neighbors and friends, stores churches — not in the way a professional map-maker would do it, but in a personal way, indicating anything which had special meaning such as a big rock by the creek, a willow tree, an abandoned wagon. Finally I said, this was not an art contest.

> During one session, for example, they made a floor plan of the inside of a childhood home, noting details such as furniture, wallpaper, floor coverings. They recalled calendars, religious pictures, pots and pans and cooking utensils, the clothesline strung behind the potbellied stove to dry the long winter underwear.

THE BEST TIME OF DAY

Fatigue can dampen memory. Consequently, says oral historian Morris Silbert, "always try to stage the interview when the subjects are at their best. If they are early morning people, don't come in the afternoon. They might be tired and want to sleep."

There is only one way to discover whether this applies to your subject: ask the person or someone who knows him or her (such as a relative or an attendant at a nursing home, etc.). Concomitant to this, you must pay extra attention to the storyteller's energy level during the interview. If you detect a drop in energy — which will likely manifest itself in less enthusiastic and descriptive answers — ask the person if perhaps it might be time to stop for a rest or for the day.

ELIMINATE DISTRACTIONS

When a memory is in full bloom, an almost magical experience can take place. The person remembering can enter a transcendent and fragile state, which has to be treated with respect and care. That means being mindful not to shatter a special or thoughtful moment in the interview with a sudden shift of direction or an inappropriate question.

Similarly, try to eliminate, or minimize, interruptions such as the phone ringing. A golden rule is UNPLUG THE PHONE. If it isn't hooked in with a jack (most are, but a few haven't yet been converted) take it off the hook and let it beep until it goes to sleep. People barging in can be prevented by a sign on the door explaining an interview is underway or by posting someone outside the interview room to ward off visitors.

PAY RAPT ATTENTION

Just as listening well supports people to speak more eloquently, so too does it benefit the flowering of memory. If the interviewee detects a lack of attention on your part, it will more than likely dampen the teller's confidence, enthusiasm, and interest. As discussed earlier in this chapter, remembering feeds off these elements, so anything that endangers them will likely cause the memory to close up or decline.

Don't underestimate how difficult it may be to maintain attention. If the teller is rambling on and on, and you don't know how to bring him or her back into focus, you can easily tune out. It happens to interviewers, including professional ones, all the time. Rather than listen, they take a mental nap. The interviewee may not betray any sign that your open-eyed snooze has been detected, but I can assure you they are aware of it far more often than the dozing interviewer thinks.

TRUTH IS RELATIVE

"I have a problem with these kinds of memoirs," a TV producer said rather accusingly after she'd interviewed me about this project. "How do you know the people will tell you the truth about their lives or their families? How do you know what they say will be objective?"

The answer is you don't and it won't. You don't know if it's "the truth," whatever that woolly beast happens to be; and it won't be objective, because nothing (TV news being a prime time example) is objective. Everything, to tell the truth, is subjective.

The producer was concerned the subject of a memoir might promote herself in a rose-colored light when, in fact, the person had a dark and uglier side that never emerged. "I have a relative who would come out looking like the greatest, most popular person in a memoir like this," she said. "But I know there are lots of things about her that are not that nice, but they'd never be exposed in the memoir."

While it's true that most, but not all, people will sugar-coat their memories to varying degrees, I don't think it should be an issue when planning or producing your memoir. Even if someone projects a false image during an interview, that persona is nonetheless part of who he or she is (sometimes a big part) and is worth capturing and preserving on tape. If the person has been playing a role for decades on end, it's doubtful you'll be able to strip the illusions in one brief interview. That goal — if you have it — is probably unachievable.

But there are some things you can do to counter a person who glosses over what you consider to be "the truth":

Be real and truthful yourself

Be careful not to expect a level of introspection and candor from your guest that you don't display yourself. If you are highly guarded, unlikely to reveal anything negative about yourself (if you were the subject of a memoir) and reluctant to share any real feelings with others, you have no right to cry foul if your subject behaves the same way.

At the same time, if your demeanor or questions project a flippant, sarcastic, judgmental or accusatory tone, don't be surprised if your subject fails to respond in an open, genuine, self-examining and introspective manner.

However, if you come across as a genuine and trustworthy person, you increase the potential for the memoir to be conducted at that same level. You can't force people to be candid or self-critical, especially if they are set in their ways, but your approach can make a difference.

Ask questions that require truthful answers

There's a natural tendency to shy away from asking sensitive or probing questions from those we're close to. But if you don't ask the question, you can't be angry with the person for not volunteering an answer that might cast the subject in a less than positive light.

Challenge an answer you know to be sugar-coated

You can do this in a playful and non-threatening way. "That's not how I remember it, dad," you might say, with laughter rather than anger in your voice. Or, "That doesn't sound right. I thought it was..." And many variations on the theme.

It's often how a question is answered that counts

You can't force a person to tell you something. Often the way a person answers — syntax, tone of voice, eye movement, body language — tells you the real answer. The camera and tape recorder capture those verbal and non-verbal moments, so you don't need to push someone to "confess all."

Interview other people

If you're really bent on getting at certain truths about events, you can interview several people about the same thing. Invariably, they will have a range of memories and opinions, which can be edited together so you and others can evaluate who is providing the most accurate version of the story.

THIS IS NOT THERAPY

As I've stated from the outset, I believe the memoir process can provide a wide range of benefits, including the opportunity to learn about yourself and those who are close to you. However, it must be approached in a way that respects everyone involved. This is not going to be easy if, for example, there are intense, hostile, or other unresolved feelings between you and your parents or caregivers.

"I think it's probably helpful to establish ground rules," says psychiatrist Dr. Ron Ruskin.:

> Even though they [the memoir tellers] are family members, and you think you know certain things, there may also be aspects of an event that you don't know. If you set the stage then everyone should be more at ease. Generally you get more information when a person is at ease.
>
> In most cases, I think you should tell the person beforehand that you're going to ask certain questions that the person might find

difficult to answer. And get their permission to do so. You need to give them a reason, so you might say, "I'm going to ask this because it's important for the sake of documentation."

If your only real purpose in recording a memoir is to confront a major problem between you and your subject, I caution you to think before proceeding, or to seek the advice of mental health professionals to determine whether this is the best time and means of dealing with the problem. It's not my position to say whether you should or shouldn't. It might work out for some people; it might be a disaster for others.

Journalist Natasha Stoynoff, the Canadian correspondent for *People* magazine, offers an example of when it seemed to have been the right decision:

> When my mother's father was sick in hospital and everyone said he was going to go, my aunt took a tape recorder to his bed and asked him all the questions that had been burning in her mind for 40 years. Like, why didn't you let me and the other girls go to school, we could have made more of ourselves if you had. She confronted him with everything. And she got answers. It was very important to her and I admire her for doing it. It's too bad, though, that we have to wait until the last minute to speak to our parents this way.

Social worker Paula David, on the other hand, is duly concerned that memoir interviewers don't play amateur psychologist:

> This is reminiscence, it's not therapy. If grandpa starts crying because [he's remembering] marital problems he had with grandma, whose been dead 40 years, this is not the time to try and fix them.

I worked with eight Holocaust survivors who had volunteered to record their memories on tape to leave a record, an archive for future generations. I was terrified at the thought of being there, terrified of hurting someone. And, that I was going to hear things I never wanted to hear. Am I going to get out of the room in one piece? Am I going to start crying when they're not crying? It was totally untread water. I've never found a book on [how to handle] this.

You have to be trained to look for psychic collapse in situations like that. This might have been the first time some of them had told their stories and you don't know what could happen. One of them said to me, "How can you go home now? Isn't your heart going to be too heavy?" I got through it, but it took an incredible amount out of me.

At the same time that she cautions against straying deliberately or inadvertently into therapy, David also encourages memoir makers to be "as emotional, personal and in-depth as possible, because the person is going to be dead and this is all you have left."

WHEN PAINFUL MEMORIES SURFACE

While operating Video Recorded Memories, I was contacted by a Polish woman, who I'll call Maria, who had survived Auschwitz. She felt that her son, who was born in Canada, did not understand her and was antagonistic. She didn't hold out hope for a reconciliation during her lifetime, but she felt compelled to leave something behind that would explain who she was and what she had gone through. "Maybe when I'm dead," she said, "he'll listen to these tapes and...."

Over several meetings, I tape recorded her life story (she didn't feel comfortable with a video camera). She had grown up in numbing poverty in Poland, so stark that she cried upon recalling the deprivation. The entire process was an emotional experience for me for I had never spoken directly to a Holocaust survivor before. Many things remain in my memory, but two stand out the most. I gave her all the copies of the tapes so I can't offer this as a verbatim quote, but the essence I can vouch for:

> We were taken by train to Auschwitz and then marched down toward the opening of the camp. As we walked along we saw these crazy people begging us to give them our clothes, our shoes and anything else we had with us. "They'll take them all away from you!" they screamed at us. We didn't pay them any attention because they had their heads shaved and looked like skeletons and were obviously crazy. We didn't know that before long we would be just like them too.

> Some time later they herded all the women into a room and divided us into two lines. A voice inside me kept saying I was in the wrong line. So when the guards weren't looking I snuck across to the other one. I and the women in that line were eventually sent to work in an ammunitions factory in Germany. I'm quite sure the others went to their immediate death.

There were many moments during my conversations with Maria when she was overcome with sadness and emotion. I tended to say nothing during these moments, until I felt she was ready to continue. Then I'd ask her if she wanted to break or proceed, leaving it entirely up to her. She always wanted to continue. Despite my experience as an interviewer, I never found any of those moments easy, nor did I feel certain I had done the "right" thing. I simply tried my best, based on what I understood to do when a deep and painful memory surfaces.

Don't be afraid to say nothing

There is a tendency, in emotional moments, to find the right words, or to make everything return to "normal." Often what results is an inappropriate or trite remark. If in doubt, remain silent but very present in your silence. When the time seems right, ask how the person is feeling, whether he or she wants to continue, needs a glass of water, etc.

Don't try and stop them

Your uncomfortableness could be such that you want to change the subject or otherwise keep the person from continuing. If the door to a painful memory has opened up, you must let the person experiencing it determine whether he or she needs to speak more about it or prefers to move on. If you invoke closure on the discussion, it could leave the person feeling agitated and anxious.

Don't minimize

"Let them deal with it," says psychologist Dr. Jane Dywan. "Don't say, 'Now, now, dear, it's okay.' Don't minimize or condescend, because some people have been through great tragedy. Never say, 'Oh, it wasn't that bad.' If they cry, let them cry. And after they seem to have [regained composure] ask them how they got over the experience, how they mastered it. Rather than leaving them feeling overwhelmed."

VERY SHY PEOPLE

Some people are so shy they refuse to allow a camera or tape recorder anywhere near them. Although you must respect their right to say no, try one last option. Ask if they'd be willing to sit down with someone else they feel comfortable with — under no obligation to talk — while you record a conversation with the other person. If the shy person agrees, see if you can then draw him or her into the discussion after a few minutes or so.

5
AN EXPERT VIEW ON MEMORY

Lull'd in the countless chambers of the brain,
Our thoughts are linked by many a hidden chain;
Awake but one, and lo, what myriads rise!
Each stamps its image as the other flies.

Alexander Pope

Dr. Jane Dywan has a Ph.D in clinical psychology and specializes in the study of human memory. She teaches the Psychology of Aging at Brock University, serves as a consultant to the Niagara Rehabilitation Centre in St. Catharines, Ontario, and is editor of the book *Neuropsychology and the Law.*

PM: Are there things you can do to help people remember events from their lives, especially elderly people?

JD: First of all, be sure that the interview is taking place without unnecessary distraction, so the person is comfortable and there aren't other people around and the telephone isn't on and you can't be disrupted by calls. And second, hearing is a problem for some older adults. To compensate for this, we often shout when speaking to them. This is not a good idea. While it is important to keep the volume of one's voice up — being careful not to let it drop too much at the ends of words and sentences — it is never good to shout because this distorts the sounds, changes the shape of your mouth and makes it harder for a person to comprehend what you are saying.

PM: What about volume?

JD: Maintaining the appropriate volume is important if the individual is suffering from conductive hearing loss, but for many older adults the problem lies not so much in the ability to hear the sounds but to process them quickly enough. What we need to do is slow down our rate of communication.

PM: How fast you speak?

JD: Yes. As some people age, the brain doesn't respond as quickly to information as it once did. The inhibitory processes are not as efficient so that stimulation from one word can still be reverberating through the system while you are speaking the next word. That reverberation can block the processing of the next word. Because processing time slows down it is important to leave enough space between words. Don't overdo it so that your speech sounds artificial. Just speak in well modulated tones at a moderate pace.

PM: Could you elaborate on "pace?"

JD: What you do is pay attention to the person's response to your communication and adjust the pacing of your words accordingly. Pace your ideas, too. Deal with one idea or issue at a time. Wait for a response or acknowledgment before you go on. Be prepared to repeat what you have just said as part of the natural flow of conversation. Be careful not to seem impatient. Relax and enjoy the interchange.

PM: Does the pitch of the interviewer's voice make a difference?

JD: If a woman interviewer has a high-pitched voice, she might want to try and drop her voice a little. When older adults have a hearing loss, higher tones are often harder to hear, so they will miss some parts of the communication.

PM: This can be compounded, I guess, if the interviewer is nervous and, out of the nervousness, speaks faster.

JD: That's right. When we are nervous we tend to speak at a higher pitch and faster as well. So we make it doubly difficult for the older adult to fully comprehend what we are saying. When we are anxious, silences seem longer and we try to fill in the spaces. Silences are important for everyone, especially older adults because it allows time to process what they have heard and to formulate their response. Silences are not necessarily empty.

PM: How would you know if you were speaking at an appropriate speed or volume?

JD: This question raises an important issue with respect to age-related changes in hearing, comprehension, memory, or any other aspect of information processing. Individual differences in older people are greater than in any other age group. These are due to differences in the health of the nervous system as well as to the enormous range of innate abilities and life experiences and training the person has had. So, while some older adults will require a slower pace, others will be very quick and very, very facile. The interviewer may have trouble keeping up. In each case, you have to feel your way along so you don't bore the person who is quick or overwhelm the person whose information processing has slowed down.

PM: Is it helpful if the person you're interviewing can see you?

JD: Absolutely. It is always a good idea to sit so that your face is fully visible. Make sure you sit with light on your face so the person can really see your lips and facial expression so they can make use of as many nonverbal clues that they might need.

PM: Most people assume that memory is sort of like a large storage area that you access. Do we know what memory is?

JD: Memory is not a big storage area with short-term memory in one bin and long-term memory in another bin. Memory simply doesn't operate that way. When we remember things, recollect them, it is inevitably a reconstruction. Memories are not stored on some kind of [internal] videotape.

PM: What does that mean?

JD: Let me give you an example. If I were to ask you about your wedding day, you would at first perhaps recollect a few images. They might come quite quickly. Then, on the basis of those, you would reconstruct other aspects of these old memories. You would have to activate the systems within your brain that experienced the experiences in the first place.

PM: How do you do that?

JD: The exact mechanisms are not understood. However, what seems to happen is that as we try to image the events we are trying to recall, such as the wedding, others follow. You first recollect that it was summer and that it was in the garden. This alone will provide many clues that will lead to other memories. You might recall that a grandparent was there and that the grandparent had driven down with a favorite uncle, etc. One moves from memory to memory through a semantic network of experiences and ideas. The event never comes back as a whole and it is rarely entirely correct.

PM: It isn't a tape.

JD: No. You cannot rewind and rerun it. Every time you recollect it, it will be somewhat different. It is a reconstruction.

PM: Are there ways a questioner can help stimulate memory?

JD: Definitely. Let's say you want them to remember something very specific, a particular incident at the wedding. You would begin by letting them tell you about whatever comes to mind for them first. Then start to ask open-ended questions that prompt the person to remember more details. "What part of the summer was it? What was the weather like that day? What could you see from where you were sitting?"

PM: You must be careful not to lead.

JD: It's very important these prompts not suggest an answer. For example, you would not say, "Well, if you were sitting there you must have been able to see the children playing on the front porch." What can happen with this sort of question is that your suggestions can get integrated into the reconstruction. The person is able to image a plausible suggestion into the narrative and it becomes part of the "memory." It might also become part of the "memory" the next time the person tells the story even though the suggested event never actually happened.

PM: It's my experience that there comes a time during a long reminiscing interview in which a person's memory gets more into full bloom. Is that a real concept?

JD: It is. It's because what you're doing is activating associations that have been formed at various times in the person's life. You are allowing the person to re-experience those events, to connect with the feelings as well as the details. Each feeling, each detail can lead to others, providing a richer and richer experience.

PM: If you make the environment more stimulating, make the event seem important, will that help stimulate the memory?

JD: If you make the session more enjoyable, if you're very responsive and nod and encourage, that's not memory [stimulation], that's social psychology. There is evidence, though, that if you're in a very sad, unhappy mood you're more likely to remember sad and unhappy events. Conversely, if you're in a happy mood, you're more likely to remember happy events.

PM: Am I right in assuming that chronological progression will help memory more than going all over the place?

JD: Depends on what you're after. If it's a conceptual thing you're after, it may not be. If it's a life story, it probably is.

PM: Any final comments?

JD: I want to really emphasize how important it is not to be judgmental. With older people, they might repeat themselves, and it's essential you don't act bored or impatient and say "Yeah, yeah, you already told me that." Instead, if you want to keep the flow going you can say, "Yes, that's right — and then what happened?" And you just have to accept that it might take longer to interview an older person because of this garden path they go off on called repetition. One other thing. Inevitably you're going to run into some older people who are beginning to have problems like early Alzheimer [disease] and strokes. If it seems that as you press for information, they start to become anxious or very repetitive, maybe it's better to back off. Memory impairment can be very serious, very real, so I'd always err on the side of caution.

And one last thing. There is a tendency to talk to older adults as if you were talking to children. This plays havoc with the older adult's self-esteem and the interviewer will be unable to achieve the mutuality necessary to support the process of reminiscence.

6
INTERVIEWING:
BEFORE THE QUESTIONS

I go as a portrait painter goes, not as a photographer. I'm interpretive. I try to get inside the character...very deeply.

Gay Talese (on interviewing)

This chapter and the next are about painting portraits of human lives and times by asking questions and following up on the answers. Like all art forms, interviewing is harder to do well than it may appear at first glance. A small number of fortunate people are naturals at engaging others in animated and structured conversation. Most are not, and discover interviewing to be a challenging process to master. If you wish to explore the art of asking questions in greater detail, I suggest reading my book *How To Interview*, (also published by Self-Counsel Press). Some of the material in this chapter originally appeared in *How To Interview*.

Whether you find interviewing easy or demanding, I guarantee one benefit: an interview will always teach you something about life as long as you keep your ears and eyes truly open. I consider it a privilege to be given permission to explore ideas and feelings with another human being in the kind of intimate circumstances characteristic of many interviews. I hope you will consider it a privilege too, because appreciation breeds respect, both for the process and its participants.

I have previously said that this book is not a technical manual; nor is it a course on the journalistic interview. This chapter has been designed for the novice, although experienced interviewers should find it helpful too. My goal is to give you information and insight to make your interviews as successful as possible. No matter what level of comfort or skill you acquire as an interviewer, you should feel a proud sense of achievement for every interview completed. It takes a certain courage and forthrightness just to do an interview. That puts you far ahead of the countless others who say they will, "one day," but never do.

CONVERSATIONAL IDEAL

"What you want to do," says Studs Terkel, "is make [the interview] a form of conversation."

"Question-and-answer doesn't work as far as I'm concerned," says Barry Broadfoot. "When I go into a stranger's home, I talk to them."

These two masters of oral history, veterans both of thousands of "conversations," are absolutely correct. The ideal interview should indeed wear the cloak of a relaxed and natural-sounding conversation. That's why it's recommended to substitute the word "interview" with "conversation," "discussion," or "talk" when proposing the memoir concept to a relative.

My experience learning the craft of interviewing, and subsequently teaching it to journalism students for more than 15 years, tells me, however, that attaining the conversational ideal is not so easy. It takes experience, know-how, and confidence. That's why I strongly urge you to plan objectives and prepare questions for each interview. The results should be twofold: your interviews will be better, and your interviewing ability should steadily improve.

As you become familiar and comfortable with the interview dynamic, you will naturally evolve your techniques toward the conversational ideal that Terkel and Broadfoot recommend. Embrace it if it comes to you quickly. Don't despair if it takes time to accomplish — many late-blooming interviewers turn out to be the best.

TRUST AND RAPPORT

"I've always thought the only way to have a successful interview is to be trusted and liked by the person you are interviewing," says journalist and author June Callwood. "Everybody, if they like you, will tell you more." Oral historian Morris Silbert champions the same philosophy. "The first thing I do is develop a rapport," he says. "If I don't have rapport [with the interviewees], I'm going nowhere."

I resoundingly agree with this valuable advice, but why is it so? Why should trust and rapport take on such important dimensions? The answer can be found if you take a moment to sit in the interviewee's chair, so to speak, on the other side of the camcorder or tape recorder.

For many people, being asked questions, whether it's coated as a conversation or laid bare as an interview, is unnerving. The degree of discomfort or self-consciousness depends on each individual and each set of circumstances. In *The Art of Interviewing for Television, Radio and Film,* author Irv Broughton quotes Jacques Lalanne, President of L'Institut de Développement Humain, in Quebec, on the origins of this commonly shared apprehension:

> It is no surprise that questions make most of us feel uneasy. They remind us of times we'd rather forget. As children, before we learned the smaller skills of excuse and evasion, questions were often a prelude to accusations, advice, blame, orders, etc. At home, we'd be asked what we did or didn't do, and one seemed designed to ferret out what we didn't know rather than what we did.

In other words, being asked questions can be scary.

In addition to personal psychology, there are other understandable reasons why people you want to interview might harbor nervousness or misgivings. Most noteworthy is the fear of public speaking. In *You Are the Message*, Roger Ailes, media adviser to U.S. presidents Ronald Reagan and George Bush, cites the results of a poll of human fears:

> Twice as many people were more afraid of speaking in public than of dying. I believe that fear of failure and embarrassment are the biggest reasons people don't do certain things in life — including speaking in front of an audience.

That multitudes of people consider death more appealing than public speaking rarely shocks anyone to whom I quote that idea. You usually don't have to look farther than your own reflection in the mirror to find someone who empathizes with the dread feelings that survey exposes. Curiously, far less compassion is usually granted the person facing a camcorder or tape recorder, especially if it's the first time he or she has ever been recorded. Being interviewed is not the same as delivering a speech or leading a group presentation, but it can evoke similar tremors of anxiety. Usually the degree is less intense than that brought on by public speaking, but it's there in some fashion nevertheless.

At the root of someone's nervousness about being interviewed are concerns worth identifying:

- Making a fool of yourself
- Saying the wrong thing
- Not knowing an answer
- Being asked a question that embarrasses you
- Saying something that will hurt or upset someone else
- Looking unattractive on camera
- Sounding "funny" on tape

- Wondering who will see/hear the tape

That's not a definitive list but it should illustrate the need to establish trust and rapport with the interviewee before embarking on the "pas de deux" of questioning. Unless these concerns are addressed and resolved, the interview may not succeed or achieve its highest potential.

How, then, do you establish trust and rapport? You must devise your own style, because genuineness is the foundation upon which trust and rapport are built. The following guideposts may help your quest.

Don't rush

If someone is nervous or distrusting, you will likely exacerbate those tensions if you rush the process. A rushed interview is one where you don't take the time to make your guest comfortable and relaxed.

If the guest doesn't know you well, that means you may have to spend some time speaking about yourself, until a point where a trusting relationship is formed. That doesn't necessarily take a long time, it just takes as long as necessary. The obvious conversation topics are family ties, your interest in the memoir project, your biography, etc. It's neither fair nor logical to assume the guest should open up for the camcorder or tape recorder while you remain hidden and protected, so to speak.

If the guest knows you well, don't make the mistake of being familiar and assume there's no need to make him or her comfortable. You should also take your time with members of your immediate family — sometimes more, because people are often most nervous in front of those they're closest to.

Understand the need for control

Nothing seems to give humans the willies more than losing control of their circumstances. Awareness of that normal need puts you in a position to compensate for it prior to the interview.

Interviewees feel a loss of control, consciously or unconsciously, as soon as they give permission for a taping. In their mind, you hold most, if not all, the cards. You decide the questions, choose what answers to follow up and what to bypass, operate the equipment, and do as you please with the finished product. (Within the law, of course. For example, if you charge money for showing or distributing the tape — for profit rather than just to cover your costs — it would be wise to obtain release forms granting you permission to do so from the people you interview.)

Explain the purpose of the interview clearly

To reduce that feeling of lost control — I'm not sure it's ever truly eliminated — return as much of it as you deem necessary or acceptable to accomplish your goals. You can do this if you clearly explain the purpose of the interview.

It has never failed to amaze me the number of times I've thought someone understood the purpose of an interview only to discover, upon final check, that it was not actually clear. Make sure you patiently and thoroughly go over the reason for the interview, encourage questions about the process, and double-check that everything spoken is understood.

Unless the interview happens immediately following your initial request and explanation (which is rare), repeat the entire process when you meet to actually do the interview. I usually say in this pre-interview stage: "I know we discussed the reason I wanted to talk with you several weeks ago, but I always like to go over it again before we start." Before the buttons are pushed, my last comment is always: "Have you any questions, concerns, anything you want to talk about before we start recording?"

Provide areas for discussion beforehand

This offers the greatest return of control. A person who doesn't know what is going to be asked often worries and imagines the worst. This is especially the case for those with little or no experience being interviewed. If you provide clear and detailed information in advance, the interviewee should be more relaxed and better prepared come taping time.

In some cases, guests may ask for specific questions. Journalists shy away from this for several reasons. One is that people have a terrible tendency to prepare and memorize answers if they know the questions beforehand, which makes the interview sound horribly artificial.

A second is that interviewers know they can't anticipate all the questions they'll ask. Most questions evolve from previous answers. But if guests expect, and have prepared for, only the points itemized in advance, a spontaneous question can catch them off guard.

A third reason is that unexpected questions can elicit interesting responses. "With people who are great off-the-cuff, you wouldn't want to spoil the surprise of their reaction to a certain question," says Daphne Ballon of Atlantis Films. "You could ask them questions that might freak them out in a good way, make them laugh or jolt them in some way."

I lay these arguments on the table when explaining to interviewees why I prefer not to supply a definitive list of questions. But I quickly add that I'm more than happy to go over what I want to accomplish with the interview, and what sorts of areas I intend to explore. They usually see the logic and withdraw their request.

There are occasions where providing questions is the only means of assuring the interview. Exceptionally nervous or elderly guests may otherwise find a memoir interview too intimidating without a specific list. By all means submit your questions but attach a caution and a proviso: "Please do not memorize answers. Be aware that some questions may arise that are not on the list."

Let them know they can make a mistake

I agree with Roger Ailes that fear of making a mistake can have a crippling affect on individual creativity. If people perceive they have only one chance to be accurate or articulate during an interview, they can become fearful and tense, which, ironically, often leads to them making more mistakes. "Don't worry if you make a mistake," I assure people beforehand. "Just stop and correct yourself or ask to start the answer over again."

If you intend to edit the interview, let them know their initial comments can be removed. "Because I can edit this, which means I can take out parts of the interview when it's over," I explain, "I'll tidy the tape up by taking out the answers that didn't work or that you didn't like."

If you aren't going to edit, I think it's preferable to have some repetition or correction on the tape than to deprive the interviewee of the freedom to have a second crack (or third or fourth, for that matter, unlikely as that may be) at an answer. Just say, in a natural manner: "If you want to try that answer again, please go ahead."

Let them know they can stop anytime

"I would think the key in dealing with someone you personally care about is that they can stop it at any time," says Daphne Ballon. "They are not a victim. Theoretically with video [and audio] they can say it 14 times. What's the sweat. It doesn't cost anything extra [to start over]." The easiest way to do this is to stop the tape, rewind over the part that didn't work, and record over it.

Negotiate what happens with the final product

"They should be able to contract what is done with the tape," says Paula David of the Baycrest Geriatric Centre. "If they really can't stand it, or it embarrasses them, make a deal that it's put in a safety deposit box for a couple of years. Then they can take a look at it and see if they've changed their mind. But don't destroy it. Don't make that an option."

Make sure the interviewee is comfortable with the technology

For some people, the memoir interview will be their first time on camera or being taped. If the subject exhibits undue nervousness about the equipment, you might try some dry runs prior to taping. "Consider annoying them with the camcorder for a couple of weeks beforehand," says David Stringer, host of "Successful Home Video." "They'll start to get used to having it around and seeing themselves." Paula David agrees that with video equipment familiarity can breed contentment. "The camcorder is a new machine to a lot of older people," she says, "so what we did was hook it into the television set, which people are comfortable with, and let them see themselves."

PREPARING THE INTERVIEW

There are two general preparation strategies to consider: identifying a set of objectives for the interview and preparing a list of questions.

You should establish, either in writing or in your mind, the principal objectives you want to accomplish in each interview. This exercise is exceptionally helpful and will improve the quality of your interviewing in two ways: one, by forcing you to think about what you're going to talk about in the interview beforehand; two, by relaxing you (as was discussed in chapter 2 concerning the benefits of research). A prepared interviewer is a more relaxed interviewer. The more relaxed you are, the better able you'll be to function with a clear and composed head in the heat of the interview.

The degree of detail is up to you, but at minimum your objectives should outline the broad areas you intend to cover. For an interview that covers the full span of your grandmother's life, they might look something like this:

- Early Years — life on farm; school days; daily activities; memories of her parents and grandparents, etc.

- Leaving Home — why she moved to Winnipeg; where she lived; jobs; etc.

- Marriage/Family — how she met grandpa; birth of her children; family outings/entertainment; family accomplishments; etc.

- Depression Years — how they survived; examples of poverty; what they did for money; how it changed their lives; funny/sad experiences; when did it end; etc.

- War Years — grandpa enlisting; what it was like with him away; his letters back home; how the children did without him; what he told her about the war; his accomplishments in the war; grandpa coming home; etc.

- Quilting — how she learned; what she's done; her special techniques; her best quilts; why she likes doing it; how she found time; etc.

- Her Children — what they have done with their lives; triumphs and tribulations; illness; careers; them leaving home; grandchildren; etc.

- Closing Thoughts — looking back on her best and worst moments; what has she learned; dreams achieved and not achieved; philosophy of life; what she'd like to say to future generations.

The decision on whether to prepare a long list of specific questions (see chapter 8 for examples) is entirely up to you. If you're not a confident or experienced interviewer, I think it's a good idea.

Should you take the list with you into the interview? Preferably not. The ideal, as suggested, is to engage your guest in a natural-sounding conversation. Reading questions off a list isn't the best way to achieve that. On the other hand, you're not a professional interviewer, and if the list gives you comfort and enables you to cover areas that otherwise you'd leave out, then by all means take it with you. My suggestion is to have it in your pocket and see if you can get by without referring to it. Perhaps retrieve it at the end to see if you've missed any important points. If so, record a final segment of "loose ends."

If you decide not to write out questions in advance, at least deliberate on the wording of three types of questions: the first question, sensitive questions, and the last question.

The opening question

How you start influences the rest of the interview. Know what you're going to begin with. "When in doubt, like in pinochle and bridge, lead with your trump," says Studs Terkel. "That means, ask about their childhood. That's always a good jumping off point."

The wording of sensitive questions

If you've decided to ask certain delicate or sensitive questions, make sure you know how to word them before the interview. It's too risky to try and find the right words in the heat of the interview. Through your awkwardness, you might unwittingly say the wrong thing.

A closing question

You want each interview to seem complete. This is best accomplished by having a closing question(s) prepared. For example: "We've covered a lot of ground during the past hour, mom, and I'd just like to bring it to a close by asking if you have any message you'd like to give to the generations that will watch this in the years ahead?" There are infinite variations, but having one at the ready will serve you well.

7

INTERVIEWING: ASKING QUESTIONS

Questions are never indiscreet. Answers sometimes are.

Oscar Wilde

Barry Broadfoot and Studs Terkel, two gurus of oral history know what they're talking about, which is not about talking. When asked to pinpoint the key to successful interviews, both unhesitatingly said listening. In Broadfoot's words, "The best historian is the best listener — always." And Studs Terkel says, "Basically, it's just listening to people."

LISTENING

If listening isn't the weakest human communication skill, I can't imagine what is. What else do we do more poorly? How many times have you been introduced to someone and forgotten the person's name immediately? How many times have you vowed never to commit such an insult again — after all, what is more important than a person's name — and done it again the next time?

The importance of listening cannot be underscored. I doubt anything turns off a speaker more than the realization that the interviewer isn't listening. A sense of betrayal, anger, and contempt can result, although perhaps masked on the surface. It can cause the interview to go downhill quickly, often with the interviewer oblivious to the reason.

Conversely, nothing is more stimulating for a speaker than to be listened to with an interviewer's complete heart and soul. I believe strongly that the more deeply you listen, the more eloquently people will likely speak. Just as an actor playing Hamlet would have great difficulty delivering a soliloquy with feeling if the audience were distracted and talking out loud, an interviewer who does not pay complete attention to what a guest is saying can diminish the interviewee's ability to speak and the quality of what he or she says.

The rewards of listening deeply are endorsed by Alex Haley, author of *Roots*, who was also an accomplished interviewer (he interviewed Malcolm X, Martin Luther King, Jr., Cassius Clay — later to become Muhammad Ali — and others for *Playboy* magazine). "What I'd find the most valuable thing about interviewing was what one might call 'the ear' — you know, to hear in depth," he told Brian Denis in *Murderers and Other People*, a collection of interviews with interviewers.

This is not the forum for exploring the whys of listening deficiencies. Instead, let's examine some possible ways to improve this vital skill:

Will yourself to listen

A concise, but powerful, point: you have to make a conscious effort to listen. Remind yourself prior to an interview to listen intently. If you catch yourself not listening, snap out of your distraction and refocus. Make listening a priority, along with knowing what to ask and making sure the tape is recording.

Accept your role

The interviewer's role is to listen, ask the right questions, keep the discussion focused, and provide other functions necessary to ensure a successful interview. It is not to show how much you know or to buffet your ego.

American humorist Fran Lebowitz has observed that for many people, listening is basically waiting for the other person to stop talking. This is destructive behavior for an interviewer.

Understand it's hard work

Active listening requires all your energy, so if you're tired or distracted, your ability to listen may diminish. "I can go out and interview someone and that person will have the sense of being with someone who is uncommonly comfortable," says Roy MacGregor, columnist with the Ottawa *Citizen* and one of Canada's top feature writers. "But I go out of the interview completely exhausted. Inside I am churning so fast, it's as if I'm playing 19 games of squash. I'm just beat."

Disturbing content may affect your listening

A normal reaction to hearing something intensely emotional or unpleasant can be to stop listening. While understandable, nothing could be worse for the speaker. Not only is it insulting, the person probably needs your support more at that point than at any other time in the interview.

As much as possible, anticipate potential emotional topics that could arise in an interview. For example, if you know the storyteller is a Holocaust survivor, has lost a child or partner prematurely or tragically, or has gone through some other intense experience, you should be prepared for deep emotions to surface. Even if you don't intend to ask about these matters, the teller may introduce them.

If you're not sure you'll be able to handle the intensity of the feelings or know what to do if the teller becomes visibly upset or agitated, seek advice from someone with experience in such matters. Sometimes just acknowledging your own vulnerability will give you the strength to hang in there if the going gets a little raw, as it sometimes can.

You won't miss important follow-ups

When reviewing the completed memoir, you don't want to discover that, because you weren't listening during an answer, a vital follow-up question wasn't asked. Now that may happen — it does to all interviewers, including the most experienced — but it will be the exception rather than the norm if you make every effort to listen actively.

A FEW RULES

The rules of successful interviewing are short, simple, and self-evident:

- Ask one question at a time.

- Ask a question that requires an answer other than yes or no. (See the section **ANECDOTE AND EXAMPLE,** below.)

- Don't answer the question for the guest. Example: Q: "I guess you were really happy when you won the lottery." A: "Yes." Let the person describe the feeling by asking: "What did you think/feel/say when you realized you'd won the lottery?"

- Listen to the answer with all your concentration.

- Decide whether an answer requires follow-up. (See the section **FOLLOW-UPS,** below)

- Display interest and enthusiasm for what the speaker says.

- Remember you can't cover everything.

- Never ask someone to be funny. (I've met few who could, under that pressure. Instead, ask about situations and let the humor evolve naturally.)

- Be mindful of your guest's energy level. As stated before, be sensitive to when the interview should come to an end.

FOLLOW-UPS

Good interviewing requires following up on some answers and not on others. How do you decide when to explore an answer further or when to move on? To some extent it's instinctive, but your instinct sharpens with experience and knowledge. In all cases, it demands that you listen carefully to the answers. These pointers should help:

- If an answer is incomplete, ask other questions until it either becomes clear or becomes obvious that clarity on this point will never be achieved.

- If an answer is interesting but it seems there's more that can be said, pursue the question.

- If the interviewee is rambling and the answer is not providing interesting material, find a way to shift to the next question.

- If the interviewee is uncomfortable with the question and it's not imperative to pursue the point further, interrupt and shift to the next question.

ANECDOTE AND EXAMPLE

Memoir is a form of storytelling. Your objective should be to elicit as many anecdotes and examples as possible. If you ask someone what it was like during the Depression, the answer might be: "It was really rough." But "really rough" doesn't tell us much. You need to follow up by asking for elaboration, in the form of stories, etc. Some speakers are not natural storytellers and this may not be easy for them, but you can help them, and the gifted talkers, by these kinds of prompts:

- What do you mean by that?

- Can you give me an example?

- Could you describe, in further detail, what you just said?

- Do you know any stories about what you just told me?

THE POWER OF SILENCE

Do not be afraid of silence. Because your adrenalin is fired up during an interview, even the briefest pause — broadcasters call it "dead air" — can seem eternal, and you will be sorely inclined to jump in and fill it with a comment or the next question. Try not to.

Let the moment breathe and see what happens. Invariably the speaker continues. The after-thoughts and elaborations that ensue are often the most illuminating of the interview.

An added bonus: If you are stuck without a next question to ask, which happens, say nothing (as opposed to babbling away in search of something to say, which also happens). In most cases the guest will continue the conversation, letting you off the hook.

TONE OF VOICE

How you ask questions is just as important as what you ask. But many of us aren't tuned in to the tones of our voice. Be mindful not to sound condescending, insincere, harsh, or judgmental. The goal is to find the appropriate tone for each question.

FLOW

A taped interview should involve a flow of questions and answers. In other words, one person shouldn't do all the talking, non-stop. Naturally, the subject should do most of the talking but, ideally, there should be an exchange between the interviewer and the interviewee. It's more interesting for the audience if the conversation moves back and forth.

INTERRUPTION

To achieve flow, it may be necessary to interrupt the subject from time to time. Most interviewers find this awkward. But it has to happen and you're the one responsible for doing it. The wording of an interruption is usually a variation on one of the following:

- "I'm sorry to interrupt but because we only have a certain amount of time I wanted to make sure we also covered (fill in the blank)."

- "Excuse me for interrupting but I really want to follow up on something you said a few minutes ago...."

BRIDGING

If a guest is rambling, on a tangent, or otherwise not following the direction of your questions, you can pull the person back on focus by what is called "bridging." This is the process whereby you create a verbal "bridge" from an answer to your next question in order to maintain the apparent flow and connection of the interview.

For example, you might say, at the end of a long answer that was not on the topic (or as part of an interruption):

- "That was an interesting story about your farm days in the Midwest, but what I'd really like to do now is focus on the years when you moved to the coast."

- "I'd like to discuss your most recent memories later on, but at the moment I'd like to talk more about your days growing up in the Yukon."

SEVERAL INTERVIEWEES

For interviews with several people at once there are two major considerations: that you make sure they are all within microphone or camcorder range, and that you act more as moderator and traffic director than as interviewer.

Ensuring that all interviewees can be picked up by your equipment can be tricky. "At a family reunion one time we started talking about our parents and we tried getting it on video," says Joyce Stephenson. "My husband was doing the camera and he found that somebody would start telling a story but he would be on the other side of the room and couldn't always get over in time to get a good picture and sound. So a lot was lost. It's got to be something that's set up."

The best policy is to arrange where people need to sit prior to recording, and to do a test before starting. For a group of three or more, seat them in a semi-circle and position yourself on the floor in the middle, kneeling or sitting down. This allows you to move the tape recorder or camera from speaker to speaker in a quick and unimpeded motion.

As "moderator" of the group, ensure that everyone, including the shy ones, get a chance to speak. Direct questions to each person: "We haven't heard from Frank yet; what was your experience during the war, Frank?" Keep people from talking over one another: "Hold it a second, hold it a second. Everyone can't talk at once. Let's hear from Alice first."

IF IT'S NOT GOING WELL

If the interview is not progressing well, especially if you think it's because the subject is nervous or upset, it's best to turn off the recorder and discuss the reason. I always turn the focus on to myself, no matter what I think may be the problem. For example:

- "I've turned off the machine because I sense you're not comfortable with the interview. Have I done or said something that has upset you?"

- "I've turned off the machine because I thought it might be a good time to take a break. Is there anything I can do, before we start again, to make the interview more enjoyable for you?"

8

SAMPLE QUESTIONS

I don't let my mouth say nothing my head can't stand.

Louis Armstrong

No one can provide you with a list of the "right" questions to ask in the "right" order. Each interview is a unique and special entity, having its own objectives, surprises, twists, and turns. As discussed in chapter 7, the best questions usually follow up on previous answers.

At the same time, I think it might be helpful for some of you to have templates — models — of the kinds of questions that might typically be asked in memoir interviews. You may never need or use these models, preferring to formulate your own questions and approach. But they might provide a launching point or confirm that the questions you've selected are on the right track.

If you do use them extensively, an obvious caveat: please modify them to the specific circumstances of your interview.

GROWING UP

These questions could typically be asked of a grandparent, parent, or any relative. They could be asked of yourself. I have supplied a large number of questions, so bear in mind the length of time you've allotted for the interview.

1. Where were you born?

2. Were you born at home? (If no, Do you know where?)

3. What is your earliest memory from childhood?

4. Do you remember the first home you lived in? (If no, What is the first home you remember?)

5. What can you tell us about that home? (Follow-ups: What size was it? How many rooms? What was it made of? Who made it? How was it heated? Where did you sleep? What was the property/garden/surrounding land like?)

6. Did any of your grandparents live with you? (If no, Where did they live?)

7. Can you tell us about them. (Where were they born? What were their full names? What did they look like? Do any of their characteristics stick out in your mind? How did they — or their families — come to North America? How did they meet? Do you know anything about their courtship/wedding/relationship? Did they get along together? How many children did they have? Did all the children survive birth? What work did your grandparents do? Did they move or stay in one place?)

8. How much do you remember about your grandparents? Did they play a prominent role in your life?

9. Were you closer to one/some of them than the other(s)?

10. Do you remember any activities you did with them?

11. Do you remember things they said to you that have stayed with you?

12. Did they tell you about what it was like for them growing up? *(Ask for details.)*

13. From them or from other sources, how much do you know about your family history? *(Depending on the answer, follow up with questions such as those suggested in 7., above.)*

14. Were your grandparents religious? Superstitious? Did they have any special skills? Accomplishments? Disappointments? *(Ask these one at a time.)*

15. Is there anything else you remember or would like to say about your grandparents before we talk about your parents? *(This is a bridging question. Notice how it moves the interview from one area of discussion to another. If the answer provides plenty of new and interesting information, you may not get to the parents for a while.)*

16. Where were your parents born? *(This may have been already answered.)*

17. What is your first memory of your mother/father?

18. What other early memories of your parents remain vivid? *(The person may give an answer from recent times rather than early days. If this happens, and your goal is to stay as chronological as possible, you might say, after the answer, "I really want to hear about the recent memories, but before we get there I'd like to go as far back as possible in your memory?")*

19. How did they meet? *(See 7. above)*

20. If you were asked to give a brief physical description and character sketch of them when they were young, what would you say. Your mother first?

21. What did your father do for a living? *(There could be various jobs, so the answer could be long or short.)*

22. Did you mother raise the children? What other work did she do? *(This could be professional or manual labor, quilting, writing, etc.)*

23. What was their goal in life? Their dreams?

24. What do you think your father and mother would have done if they hadn't been *(whatever they answered to 21. and 22.)*?

25. Were they strict with you when you were young?

26. Did they teach you any special skills *(such as music, building, knowledge of animals/nature, etc.)*

27. Did you have any pets? *(If applicable, What animals were on the farm?)*

28. Where did you go to school? *(Depending on the answer, you could explore details about early schooling such as the size of the school, the curriculum, discipline, favorite/hated teachers, chores at school, what did you like/dislike, what you wore, did you take a lunch, how far away was it, how did you get there, etc.)*

29. Did you have chores around the house?

30. What did you like doing best as a child?

31. How did you get along with your brothers/sisters? *(if applicable).*

32. Would you give their full names and dates of birth, if you know them?

33. Who were you closest to?

34. What special memories do you have of doing things with your family? *(Holidays, swimming holes, hunting/fishing, church events, etc.)*

35. Were you poor/wealthy? Examples?

36. Were there bad winters, droughts, etc., when you were growing up?

37. What did you do for fun?

38. Do you remember a Christmas/Hanukkah/other *(depending on their faith/culture)*? Birthdays?

39. What was the town/city/farm etc. like where you lived?

40. Did you have any special places that you went to?

41. What kind of a child were you? (A loner? Popular? Did you have any serious illness? Did you read, paint? etc.)

42. Were you closer to your father or mother?

43. How did you get along with them? *(This could be a sensitive area to explore, so you might want to know the answer and whether the person feels comfortable speaking about this before asking.)*

44. What were your adolescent/teenage years like? *(This might have come into previous answers.)* Did you have to leave school at an early age? What was a typical day like *(especially for people brought up on a farm)*?

45. Who was your first love? *(This could precede teenage years.)* Your first kiss? First date? Did you smoke, drink, get into trouble?

46. Did you keep a diary? *(If yes, and the teller still has it, you could have the person read excerpts from it now or, depending on your structure and whether the memoir is being edited, later on.)*

47. What did you think you would do when you became an adult?

48. What were the most significant things that happened to you during your early years, before you were 21? *(I chose 21 arbitrarily. It could be any age that marks the transition from adolescence into adulthood. For someone married at age 16, I would focus on events before 16. For someone who left home at age 18, that would likely be the demarcation age.)*

49. What was your greatest accomplishment before the age of 21? Your greatest disappointment?

50. When did you leave home? (or, Was there a point where you felt you'd become an adult?)

CAREER

I have chosen a doctor as a model for this type of interview. It can be modified for other careers such as lawyer, nurse, teacher, business person, etc. These questions can also be adapted for people who had various jobs or didn't have a specific "career" as such.

1. What was the first paying job you ever had? How did you get it?

2. How old were you?

3. How much were you paid?

4. What were your responsibilities?

5. What were your hours?

6. Did you enjoy it?

7. What other jobs do you remember doing before you started your career?

8. When did you decide to become a doctor?

9. Did you always want to be a doctor?

10. Did your parents support your career interest?

11. Why did you choose that career?

12. Had you wanted to do something else?

13. Where did you go to university/study/apprentice? (*If it was away from home:* Was it hard to leave home? Had you ever lived away from your parents before? How old were you? Do you remember the day you left? How did you get there? Did any of your friends go to the same school as well? Had anyone else in your family gone to university?)

14. Was money a problem at the time or were you okay financially?

15. What was your school experience like?

16. Was there a particular teacher you remember most? A mentor?

17. How did you do in school?

18. Did you get into any trouble?

19. What was school like then as compared to now? (Did you have to dress a certain way? Rules? Punishments? Work load? How did you address teachers? What was the teacher/student relationship like?)

20. Did you win any awards or other forms of recognition?

21. Did you participate in any extra-curricular activities?

22. Did you have any romances? *(If so, ask for details. If the romance was with his or her future spouse, you'll have to decide when to explore that in detail at this time or later part in the interview. See* **MARRIAGE AND FAMILY** *below for possible questions.)*

23. Did you start work as a doctor right after graduation? *(If no:* Why not? What got in the way? What did you do until you started practicing? What changed to allow you to start practicing?)

24. Do you remember your first day as a doctor? *(If no:* What is your first memory as a doctor?)

25. What memories do you have from the early days? *(This answer should provide many areas to explore in detail. If the subject is not forthcoming, however, you could try some of the following questions to stimulate memories/anecdotes.)*

26. What were some of the illnesses you dealt most with?

27. Did you have patients with polio? Diphtheria?

28. Do any patients or particular cases come to mind?

29. Did you make house calls? *(For doctors in rural areas:* Did you have to travel far to visit patients/families?)

30. How was it different being a doctor then than it is now?

31. What do you think was the biggest difference?

32. How hard did you work?

33. What was it like for your family, with your being on call?

34. Did the weather ever play a factor in any of the cases you dealt with?

35. Did you remember any unusual cases? *(For example:* Did you ever have to help a sick animal?)

36. How did you deal with being around people who were dying? Was it hard on you emotionally?

37. What were your proudest moments as a doctor?

38. What were your most disappointing moments?

39. If you could start over again, would you still be a doctor or would you choose something else?

40. What would you say to your grandchildren/great grandchildren/future generations in the family who want to become doctors? What advice would you give them?

MARRIAGE AND FAMILY

The following questions are based on a model of an interview with a woman (the interviewer's maternal grandmother) who spent most of her adult life raising her family while, at the same time, pursuing an interest in painting. Her marriage was a happy one. Her husband, the interviewer's grandfather, died several years before the interview.

1. When you were a little girl, did you want to get married when you grew up?

2. Did your parents have a good marriage? *(If yes:* Was that a good model for you? *If no:* Were you determined not to make the mistakes they made?)

3. Did you date/court much when you were young?

4. Who was the first boy you fell in love with? What was your first kiss?

5. How did you meet grandpa?

6. Did you like him right away?

7. What did he look like then?

8. What attracted you to him?

9. Who pursued whom? Did he go after you?

10. Did you have many suitors at the time? Was he also going out with other women?

11. How long was your courtship?

12. People courted differently then compared to now. What were the "rules" of courtship in your day?

13. Did you follow them?

14. Did your parents like him? His parents like you?

15. Do you remember the first time your parents met him? What did they say to you?

16. When was your first kiss?

17. What sorts of things would you do on a date?

18. Did you have to be chaperoned?

19. At what time did you have to be home by?

20. What did you wear on dates? Did you make your clothes?

21. What was the most daring thing you did with him before you were married?

22. Music and dancing are a big part of a modern date. Was it also that way for you?

23. What sorts of things did you do during courtship that people don't do now?

24. Who proposed to whom?

25. Describe how the proposal took place?

26. Did you say yes right away?

27. What plans did you make for your wedding?

28. Where and when was your wedding?

29. What did you wear? Did you make the dress? What did grandpa wear?

30. Who was your bridesmaid? Who was grandpa's best man?

31. What was the weather like?

32. Do you remember the ceremony? What sticks out in your mind from that day?

33. Did you go on a honeymoon? (Where to? Where did you stay? *Depending on what your grandmother is like and your relationship with her, you might ask:* Was it a romantic time? Was grandpa a romantic person?)

34. What was the first home you and grandpa had together?

35. When was your first child born? (*You will likely know the names of all/any children, and will modify your questions accordingly. So, it might be:* Tell me about my mother's birth? About Uncle John's, etc.)

36. Do you remember the first birth? Where did it take place. Was it difficult? Who was there? Did you have a midwife? Where was grandpa?

37. What was it like to hold your first baby? (*You can then explore questions about subsequent births, if applicable.*)

38. How did you decide on the name(s). Were there other choices?

39. Was it hard raising children in those days?

40. What was my mother like as a child? (What did she look like? Her temperament? First words? Easy/difficult baby?)

41. Did any of the children suffer serious illness? (*You may know if any children died in child birth or at a young age. If you don't, I recommend trying to find out before the interview.*)

42. Did you have any help raising the children? Did grandpa help?

43. What was it like raising children then, compared to now?

44. Today parents worry so much about someone, a stranger, doing harm to their children? Did you have any worries like that?

45. Give a character sketch of each child when they were young? *(You may want to just concentrate on your mother. If there were a lot of children it might not be advisable because it would take too long to sketch them all.)*

46. Were the children very different from each other? What are your favorite memories from their early years, teen years, adulthood? *(If you want to concentrate on your grandmother's memories of your mother, this area of questioning can be greatly expanded.)*

47. How much time if any, did you have for yourself?

48. When did you paint?

49. What did you paint?

50. What did painting mean to you?

51. Did you sell any? Try to? Give them away? Do they still exist? *(If yes, it would be great, for a video, to show them; for an audiotape, to have her describe one or two.)*

52. Did you ever think you could have been a professional painter?

53. Did any of the children paint? *(This is a bridging question, allowing you to flow naturally back to a discussion about the children.)*

54. What were your dreams for the children?

55. How did those dreams turn out?

56. What were the best times with your family? *(Holidays, trips, going to the cottage, etc.)*

57. What did you do for entertainment at home?

58. Were there hard times, too?

59. What was the most difficult time for you as a parent?

60. How did you and grandpa get along?

61. What was he like to live with?

62. Was it hard for you, after he died?

63. If he were here today, what do you think he'd like to say for this memoir?

64. Do you still paint? *(If no:* When did you stop? *If yes:* How often? What do you paint? What sense of satisfaction does it give you?)

65. Some people today think it's not enough of a life for a woman if she spends most of her time raising a family. Is that how you feel?

SPECIFIC ERA: DEPRESSION

Your memoir, or part of it, might focus on a specific time period such as the stock market crash of 1929, the Depression, World War II, the Vietnam War, etc. This model is for an interview with a man (your grandfather) who was 18 and living in Toronto with his family when the Depression started.

1. How old were you when the Depression began?

2. Did you know it was a "depression" at the time?

3. Where were you living?

4. What kind of work was your father/mother doing at the time?

5. How many were in your family? *(Names, ages, occupations/marriages — if applicable.)*

6. How many were at home?

7. Can you describe your home? Did your parents own it?

8. How would you describe your parents economic situation before the Depression began? (Poor, middle class, well off?)

9. What plans did you have for your own life at age 18?

10. How did the Depression affect those plans?

11. When did you know the tough times were going to last for a while?

12. How much do you remember about those "ten lost years," as they're called?

13. Were they "lost years" for you? For your parents? Brothers/sisters/friends?

14. Can you give some examples of life back then?

15. Did your father lose his job?

16. Did you have any work? Your mother?

17. What did you do for money?

18. How desperate did it become?

19. What did you have to eat? Were there times when you didn't have enough?

20. Did you follow the news, politics of the day?

21. Did you become politically involved?

22. What was Toronto like then compared to now?

23. How did you get around?

24. Did you have any luxuries?

25. What did you do for entertainment?

26. Do you remember the cost of anything compared to now? (A newspaper? Movie? Loaf of bread? Pair of shoes?)

27. The Depression is pictured as a hard and glum time. Did you also have fun? In what form?

28. What was the hardest aspect of the Depression for you?

29. What was the brightest moment?

30. Did you learn from it? Was there value in the experience?

31. What kept you going? Were you religious?

32. Some people who went through the Depression find they can't throw anything out. To this day they hoard food — waste not, want not. Are you like that?

33. Has the Depression shaped you?

34. The recent tough times in North America are sometimes referred to as a Depression. In your mind, do they compare?

35. What do you think of the Depression now, looking back all those years?

20 DIFFERENT QUESTIONS

Not all interviews need to be chronological or information-based. Here are examples of some less obvious questions you might ask or incorporate into a chronological interview.

You might ask these without notice, suggesting that the teller answers with the first thing that comes to mind. Or, you might present them in advance, to allow time for due consideration. Each has its own advantages, although my bias lies with the surprise element. I think the responses would be more interesting, less calculated for effect.

1. What person most influenced the direction of your life?

2. When were you happiest?

3. Did you ever almost die?

4. What was the best thing you ever did for someone else?

5. What are you most regretful for having done?

6. Is there a book or movie that has a significant impact on your life?

7. Did you ever meet someone famous?

8. Was there a turning point or points in your life?

9. What's the most vivid dream(s) you remember?

10. If you could add a character trait you're missing, what would it be and why? If you could subtract...?

11. If you could have married anyone in the world apart from your spouse, who would it have been? Why?

12. Pick three people from all of history to have dinner with. Why?

13. What material things would you want with you if you were on a desert island?

14. If you could have accompanied any explorer in time, who would you have gone with? Why?

15. What was the greatest idea you ever had that you followed through on? The greatest you didn't follow through on?

16. What, more than anything that you haven't tried, would you like to have done/still do?

17. Have you ever had a paranormal experience?

18. Do you believe in God? If so, what does God "look" like, if "look" is the right word?

19. Is there life after death?

20. If you had to write your obituary, what would you say?

9
TAPE RECORDER SURVIVAL BASICS

*Perhaps tape recorders are to the spoken word what
the phonograph is to music: they make it possible
for us to preserve the voices of our mothers and
fathers telling us the history of their times.*

Marc Kaminsky, *The Uses of Reminiscence*

Technology both mystifies and enthralls me. After 20 years as
a writer and broadcaster, during which time I've literally
conducted thousands of interviews with a tape recorder, I still
marvel that this small, unencumbered object can reproduce
the human voice with such clarity.

WHY USE A TAPE RECORDER?

I don't think there's any argument that the tape recorder is
less intimidating than a camcorder. "After the first few minutes they forget the tape recorder is there," says oral historian
Barry Broadfoot. "But a person who's never faced a camera
before can get mike fright, stage fright. When someone's got
the camera on them, that's the evil eye."

Although most people are far more self-conscious about
being filmed than voice recorded, the tape recorder can still
make some feel uncomfortable. To alleviate or reduce their
discomfort, consider the following:

- If the subject of your interview is staring nervously at
  the tape recorder, try to place it in a position out of his
  or her eye line. In doing so, make sure it's still within
  range of picking up the interviewee's voice clearly.

- Many people claim to have a terrible voice. "It sounds awful on tape," is a common refrain. Respond by letting them know that practically everyone says the same. "When you speak, your voice resonates through your skull and therefore you as a speaker don't hear what I hear as a listener," you can explain. "It sounds slightly different. Therefore, it's natural to be startled when you hear your voice on tape. It's unfamiliarity, surprise, nothing more than that."

- Many women claim to have too high a voice. (High voice concerns are almost always from women and are basically unfounded.) Respond by saying: "Your voice is fine. I knew what your voice sounded like before asking to do the memoir and if it were a drawback I wouldn't have asked you."

AN UNCOMPLICATED, GOOD QUALITY MACHINE

The tape recorder is easy to operate. Don't let anyone tell you different. If you can locate the record button(s), you've mastered the intricacies of most consumer machines.

Despite being uncomplicated and mechanically reliable, I've listened to all sorts of people — including professional writers — whine about tape recorders being undependable, how a priceless interview was lost because of "that damned piece of junk." For some reason unfathomable to me, the tape recorder is constantly denigrated as being complicated or prone to breaking down. It's not true. Almost every "technical" problem I've encountered or had described to me was caused by basic human carelessness. Making successful tape recordings requires a modicum of know-how. If you follow a few simple procedures, you should rarely, if ever, have a technical problem.

Cheap equipment is more likely to break down than quality equipment. Many people are reluctant to purchase a moderate- to high-quality tape recorder, perhaps because so many inexpensive machines are available in stores.

You don't have to spend a fortune to get a reliable recorder, but suffice it to say that the better the equipment the less chance it will break down and the better the quality of the recording. I can't give you an exact minimum to spend, as prices vary according to brands and when and where you shop. I would say, though, that $20 in 1993 dollars will not likely get you the quality required, while a machine in the $75 to $200 range should be more than adequate. You can obviously spend a lot more, but unless you plan to broadcast your tapes it's probably not necessary.

- Seek advice: If you don't feel competent to determine a good machine, ask a salesperson or knowledgeable friend for advice. Shop around. Compare what different dealers say to you.

- Make sure it has the right mikes: Get a machine that has both a built-in mike and a jack for plugging in an external mike. This is important because you want the option of being able to use either type of microphone. Make sure you don't buy a "tape recorder" that turns out to be a machine only capable of playing back tapes, like a Walkman. It's easy to make that mistake.

- Get a machine that operates both on batteries and AC power: This is not mandatory but well advised. Not only can you save money by using AC when batteries are unnecessary, it provides a backup source of power if your batteries run low.

- Four batteries rather than two: My experience is that a tape recorder that runs on only two batteries (especially if they are AA) might not have the juice required to make good recordings.

- Regular-size cassettes rather than microcassettes: One reason is to have the capability of dubbing or transferring the material on cassette onto a reel-to-reel tape (see chapter 11) for editing purposes. The regular-size cassettes, which professional broadcasters use, also produce better sound.

- A pause button: This is helpful when you need to stop the interview for a moment or two. A pause button lets you resume the interview at the point where you left off, with no obvious sound on the tape. If you have to rely on the stop button, it usually makes a clunking or wowing noise on the tape and often doesn't pick up the beginning of the continued section cleanly (you can miss part of the first word or two).

- Have the salesperson explain all the features: If you're not comfortable reading manuals, have the salesperson go over every function in the store before you plunk down your money. If the clerk doesn't want to, go elsewhere. Don't be rushed. Don't say you understand something until you do. Some clerks can make you feel stupid if you don't easily understand technology. That's their problem. You are not alone. We are in the millions.

CHARGE YOUR BATTERIES!

Battery failure is the number one (by a landslide) technical problem you'll encounter. Eliminate battery conk-out and the only other thing you'll likely have to deal with are acts of God. Would you embark on a long drive in your car without getting gas? Well, to a tape recorder the batteries are the gas.

The rules are simple. For an important interview, put in a fresh set of batteries. That way you know for sure they won't go dead halfway through. Take a spare set along with you.

Better still, invest in a battery charger and rechargeable batteries. For an initial modest investment, you'll save a fortune over time. Charge the batteries prior to the interview to ensure they're at capacity power.

USE THE AC POWER CORD

Using the AC power cord will make all of the above on batteries redundant. A word of warning, though. Don't assume the plug that comes with the machine, which is probably quite short, will be long enough to allow you to place the tape recorder anywhere you want. Take an extension cord with you (be wary if it's three-pronged because the wall socket may be old and not take it) and always have batteries just in case.

DON'T BUY CHEAP CASSETTES

To be safe, purchase recognizable, quality brand names. The three-for-a-dollar deals are tempting but the tape is so thin it might break during recording. On the other hand, you don't need super-expensive tapes, the kind recommended for recording music. Your manual should identify the tape characteristics for your machine. Check for "low noise," "normal bias," or "chrome" tape.

A small point: get cassettes that are screwed together (some of the cheap ones are just glued). Tape can become snarled within a cassette, which you can untangle if able to unscrew the two plastic sections.

USE 90- TO 120-MINUTE TAPES

I like to let an interview go uninterrupted for as long as possible. For that reason, I prefer 90-120-minute cassettes. However, the longer the running time, the thinner the actual tape. That's another reason I always buy quality tapes. (In 20 years I've never had a 90- to 120-minute tape break. But cheap ones might, so don't use them. It's not worth the savings!) As well, always take extra tapes with you. Nothing is worse than running out of tapes during a wonderful interview in which the subject's energy is overflowing.

DO A VOICE TEST

Doing a voice test prior to the interview will ensure the machine is recording and will provide a voice level of you and the subject. Place the recorder where it will sit during the interview. Make sure you both speak at a normal volume. A useful test is to record the date and name of the person being interviewed. Play it back to make sure everything works.

WEAR EARPHONES

If you wear earphones (an inexpensive, unobtrusive set will do), you will hear if the interview is recording. Nothing — and I mean nothing — feels worse than to do a wonderful interview and then discover it didn't record.

If you don't feel comfortable with earphones (or you don't have any with you), check the interview periodically. There's usually a natural break in the interview, such as when you turn a tape over. At that time, rewind the tape slightly to make sure it recorded. Do a similar test at the end of the interview. Even better, purchase a machine with a "record" indicator, so you can see if the record function has been activated.

If, for some reason the interview didn't record, apologize to the guest and ask if you could return at a later date to do it again (or, if the person's energy is still strong, after a short break). To make the best of a bad situation, you could say that often it's better the second time around because you've both had a rehearsal.

CLEAN YOUR MACHINE

Cleaning your machine doesn't involve much: just a swabbing of the recording heads with head cleaner (easily purchased) or rubbing alcohol (check your manual) once every dozen or so hours of usage. Ask the salesperson how to do this. Your manual will also guide you.

LABEL THE TAPES IMMEDIATELY

Labeling tapes is important. If you're using a lot of tapes, and you leave them unlabeled, you could end up recording over one by mistake.

MIKING

You want to record clearly both the subject's voice and your own. But, if you have to choose between properly miking the two, the subject's voice is obviously far more important.

An external microphone provides far superior sound quality than a built-in one and I recommend purchasing one (they're inexpensive). It's best to get an omnidirectional or bidirectional mike (as opposed to a unidirectional one), as they pick up your voice as well as the guest's.

When using an external mike, these are additional points to consider:

- Put the microphone on a stand. I recommend against holding the microphone for several reasons. One is arm fatigue. Speaking from painful experience, it doesn't take long before your arm starts to tremble if you have to hold a microphone extended for more than a few minutes. Second, by holding it, you run the risk of having mike noise, which is caused by the microphone cord moving about. Better to use an actual mike stand (which can be purchased inexpensively) or to improvise one yourself. This can be as simple as a set of books onto which you place or tape the mike.

- External mikes record best what they're pointing at. Position the mike in a position where it's aimed at both you and your guest.

- If you insist on holding the microphone in your hand, place the mike just below the subject's chin, so the speaker doesn't constantly gaze into an object as a reminder that his or her voice is being recorded. You get excellent voice pick-up and it doesn't seem to bother people as much.

- If you hold or place a microphone too close to a speaker's mouth, you create the possibility of them "popping their p's" — words beginning with "p" will have a slight exploding sound in front of them. Likewise, sibilant "s's" will become more pronounced.

- Where you sit in relation to the interviewee is critical. I find right angles work best, rather than directly opposite someone. At right angles you can sit close to someone without making him or her feel trapped or boxed in. It also allows for relaxed eye contact. Sitting directly across a table, on the other hand, can make a person feel uncomfortable and can make eye contact too frequent and intense.

- Lapel mikes, which clip on to the top of a shirt, blouse, dress or jacket can be useful and less distracting than an external mike, although few consumers use them. They tend to pick up the speaker's voice very well and the questioner's less so, sometimes hardly at all. The solution is to have a lapel mike for each of you, but that requires buying a Y-cord (if you have a mono recorder), which is inexpensive. Both lapel mikes are plugged into the two connectors on the Y-cord, which then goes into the mike jack on the recorder. A drawback of lapel mikes is their sensitivity to movements such as rustling of clothing or nervous playing with the cord, which translate on the recording as loud and distracting noises.

If you are using the machine's built-in microphone, keep in mind these points:

- Make sure the built-in microphone is facing the subject's mouth. It's usually on one corner of the machine, so have that corner pointing at the primary speaker and not you. Preferably, get into a position where it will also record your voice at a good level too.

- Choose the best place to set the tape recorder. If your subject is sitting, which will be the usual case, put the recorder on a table or some other stable object near the speaker. This may require you to move some furniture around. Don't be bashful; it's important. Don't start the interview until you are certain the machine is close enough to the storyteller and the microphone is pointing toward him or her. Be watchful, during the interview, in case the subject moves back in a chair or is otherwise "off-mike." If that happens, nudge the tape recorder closer as inconspicuously as possible.

- If you are farther away from the mike than the storyteller, compensate by asking your questions a bit louder. What you have to say is important too, not just the response. This will also be helpful to the subject if hearing impairment is a factor.

SOFT-SPOKEN ADVICE

If the person you're interviewing speaks softly, you might have to ask him or her to speak a bit louder for the microphone. However you broach this, be sensitive and use the equipment as the reason. Rather than saying, "Gee you speak so softly, could you not talk a bit louder?" which might make the person feel self-conscious, blame it on the equipment. "This microphone isn't the most sensitive and I wonder if you could help me by speaking more loudly than you normally would so it will record better."

If you know in advance the person is soft-spoken, if at all possible use an external microphone and place it closer to the person's mouth than normal. The danger with this, though, is that an external mike tends to be a bit more intimidating and intrusive, so it could have the opposite affect and make the person even quieter. If you sense that happening, switch to the built-in. In either case, try to get the recorder as close to the person, within a comfort zone, as possible.

BEWARE WHEEZING REFRIGERATORS

When tape recording, become super sensitive to ambient or background sounds. Unfortunately, most interviewers are oblivious to the sounds within the microphone's range other than the speaker's voice, and those sounds then end up on their tape.

When I worked as a radio broadcaster, whenever I did an interview on location, in other words away from our studio, my first task always was to case the location for ambient sound. I did this by standing quietly where the interview was to take place and noting every sound I could hear.

What are ambient sounds? Anything the microphone picks up, such as telephones ringing, people talking in another room, traffic, music, air conditioners (one of the worst), and loud, wheezing refrigerators. When the last two sources of white noise (air conditioners and fridges) are recorded in the background of your interview, they often cause your tape to sound as if it's malfunctioned slightly, just enough to ruin or diminish the quality of the recording.

The solution? Don't begin an interview until you're happy with the room's sound. This might require a degree of courage on your part, because you'll have to ask your subject to move to another location. Be sensitive, however, to the subject's need for a familiar and comfortable space. Moving might be a good technical decision but an unwise public relations one.

In those situations, try to find ways to diminish the offensive sounds. I've put coats over air conditioner vents, taped manila envelopes over ceiling vents, moved furniture away from noise sources, asked maitre d's to turn down Muzak, and decreed that people in other rooms remain quiet during interviews.

DESIRABLE SOUNDS

There is a tendency to want the interview location to be absolutely quiet. This is acceptable strategy but not always the best creative decision.

For example, for an interview with someone who loves nature, you might consider taping the interview outside in a garden, park, or nature area. Not only is that likely to stimulate conversation, but the ambient sound — birds singing, the wind ruffling the leaves, squirrels squawking — gives the recording a fuller, richer sound.

Be aware, however, that interviews recorded outside can be ruined by too much wind whistling through the microphone. If the wind is not too strong, this can be overcome by using a piece of foam (a wind sock, attainable from your local electronics store) or, in a pinch, by literally using a sock or some other piece of cloth to help block out the noise. Do a sound check first, though, in case the material doesn't work, or works too well and muffles the speaker's voice too.

The opposite, of course, is an ambient sound that distracts or creates a discordant message to the content of the interview. When recording the nature lover in a park, it would be annoying to have a boom box blasting out rap music at a nearby picnic.

Here are some other examples of ambient sound situations:

- A grandfather clock chiming in the background. I find this to be a beautiful sound and cannot think of an interview where it wouldn't add to the texture of the background.

- Being outside — it's a very different sound than indoors — and whether it's a gurgling brook, or just the subtle sounds of the open space, it tends to add a lovely background to your interview.

- Loud traffic. Usually distracting, unless what you're discussing has a traffic theme. If your subject is a bus driver, doing the interview at the bus depot might be a perfect location.

- Crying child. A very loud and piercing sound. Rarely, even in interviews about grandchildren, will it add to the tape. A laughing child is the opposite.

10
CAMCORDER SURVIVAL BASICS

Can you hold a loaf of bread? Can you look through a viewfinder? Can you press a button? If you answered, "Yes!" to all of the above (and you're warm-blooded), you can use a camera. Yes, they really are that simple. Just point and shoot.

Robert Wolenik

The technical gadgetry now available to home videomakers is mindboggling. Thanks to the marriage of computers with video equipment, anyone with the time, money, and inclination can produce virtually broadcast quality productions at home.

If you are not a video boffin, **DON'T WORRY. THIS CHAPTER IS FOR YOU.** I'll leave the complex and ever-changing technical advice to others far more qualified than I. There are stacks of detailed instructional books, magazines, and videos that provide excellent up-to-the-minute accounts of what to buy and how to use it. This chapter is aimed at the person with average (or beginner's) technical knowledge and interest. The following is what you need to know to shoot your video reasonably well.

KNOW YOUR CAMCORDER

This is the bottom line. Read your manual — many people don't, at least not all of it. Get help if you can't figure out any of the features.

Practice with your camcorder until you know how to operate it. At minimum you can get by with knowing how to load a tape and press record. Most camcorders are that automatic.

WATCH TV

You can enroll in a 24-hour-a-day course on camera techniques by turning on your TV set. Watch interviews on television. How are they framed? (See **FRAMING AND COMPOSITION** below). When and how often does the camera move? What is the opening or establishing shot? How are titles, narration, music, and other effects used?

By watching TV with a critical eye, you can learn the basics (as well as advanced techniques) of shooting memoirs.

PRACTICE RUNS

Perhaps the single biggest mistake amateur videographers make is not doing a practice run. "You have to play with your consumer equipment," says TV Ontario's David Stringer. "Do it before you drive to Belleville to interview your grandmother. Interview members of your family for practice. That'll tell you if you're making lighting and sound mistakes."

MONITOR YOUR WORK

It's helpful to see what you're shooting on a color TV monitor rather than just the small, black-and-white viewfinder on your camera. Not only will you gain a clear image of the exact picture being recorded, it also shows you the color and lighting quality. If the color is wonky, you can adjust before starting the interview.

Either connect your camera into your TV (your manual will explain how) or purchase a small monitor. The added benefit of a monitor is portability — most TVs are too large or valuable to lug around on a shoot.

A word of advice on where to place the monitor during the interview. My suggestion is to keep it out of the interviewee's sight line, for it's human nature to look at oneself. You don't want the storyteller's eyes staring off at the monitor. Also, if the teller can see the monitor's screen during an interview, it can make him self-conscious and uncomfortable.

TRIPOD

A tripod isn't essential (it's close to it), but it sure makes life easier on a long shoot such a memoir interview. Lightweight camcorders are very hard to keep steady for any period of time (the heavier the camera, the easier it gets). As a result, most hand-held interviews have unnecessary and distracting motion.

That isn't to discourage hand-held shots in your video. They are imperative for many locations and situations where there's action (an interview during a walk in the woods), cramped quarters (in a car) or where you want your production to have a certain stylistic (non-static) look.

CAMERA LEVEL

A common mistake is to crank up the tripod as high as possible and shoot down at a guest sitting on a chair, which dwarfs the speaker. The opposite is to shoot from below, which makes a person look unnaturally large, although a slight angle from below can be flattering. Under normal circumstances, aim the camera at eye level. Any variation should be done with a specific purpose in mind.

WHO OPERATES THE CAMERA?

For a long, sit-down interview, I strongly recommend having someone operate the camera other than the person asking the questions. "Have a second party tape the interview," agrees Dianne O'Connell in a 1990 article in *Videomaker* magazine. "Older people in particular will be more comfortable talking to a familiar face than to a camera."

If you opt for a separate camera operator, select the person carefully. Make sure the person knows the equipment (a technical rehearsal may be helpful, as cameras can differ), appreciates the sensitive nature of the interview (you don't want the operator distracting the subject, especially at critical moments), and understands how you want it shot. For example, you might say, "If grandad starts talking about when grandma died, maybe zoom in slowly for a few moments."

If the subject of the memoir doesn't know the operator personally, introduce the operator and let him or her spend a bit of time with the teller before the recording begins. Keep in mind that the teller might understandably feel self-conscious about discussing or revealing family stories in front of a stranger.

WHERE SHOULD THE INTERVIEWEE LOOK?

In most cases, the interviewee should look at whoever is asking the questions. This is further argument for using a second person to operate the camera. As mentioned above, an elderly person may not know where to look — and therefore his or her eyes might wander — if the questions are coming from somewhere behind a distant camera.

When setting the camera in position for a sit-down interview, have it pointing directly at the interviewee unless you have another deliberate camera angle in mind. Have the questioner sit facing the interviewee (as opposed to side-by-side on a couch, for example), with the camera shooting over one of the questioner's shoulders. You want to avoid a situation where the interviewee is always looking away from the camera (perhaps to make eye contact with a questioner sitting at an angle to the camera direction).

Documentary filmmakers often try to get interviewees to look directly into the camera. "It is a powerful, compelling effect," says Daphne Ballon of Atlantis Films. "But it's hard for most people to do that, and maintain it during a long interview."

THREE LITTLE SHOTS

"Basically, any story [and memoir] can be told with three camera shots," write authors Dell Dennison, Don Doman, and Margaret Doman in *Producing a First-Class Video for Your*

Business, (another title in the Self-Counsel Series). "The establishing shot or long shot (LS). The medium shot (MS). The tight shot or close-up (CU)."

The establishing shot, as the name suggests, introduces the person being interviewed and the location. For a memoir to be recorded in your grandmother's living room, you would likely begin with a long shot that shows all of her (head to toe), where she's sitting and some of the space around her (to get a sense of the room).

After staying on the long shot for a brief time (it's up to you, but I wouldn't keep it there more than a minute), slowly start to zoom in to a medium shot. This is basically a head-and-shoulders picture, with a slight distance between your grandmother's head and the top of the screen. Most of the video will be shot at this distance. It's nice to see her hands, if she's the type to move them when talking, so you want to keep the camera far enough back to include them in the frame.

At certain times you'll want to bring the camera in closer for a tight shot. In a close-up, the interviewee's face is basically full-screen. This shot is typically employed during emotional or sensitive moments, when you really want to see the person's eyes and facial gestures.

Be careful not to overdo close-ups. If the interviewee is undergoing a particularly difficult moment — perhaps crying — it may be a better decision to slowly pull the camera back from a close-up to a medium shot. Holding a tight shot in these kinds of moments can make viewers feel uncomfortable, as if they are violating the person's dignity. A good rule for close-ups is to use them sparingly and with consideration for both the subject and the viewer.

Finally, move the camera in response to what is taking place. If the teller is making animated gestures with her hands, for example, make sure you capture this in frame. Don't remain locked in a certain shot if the action dictates a different one.

DON'T OVER ZOOM

There is a seemingly irresistible temptation to over zoom. "People think that because it's there, they have to use the zoom feature," says David Stringer. "I use a zoom when a person changes gears [in something they say or do], so that I change gears of my shot, too. You also don't have to use the whole 10 to 1 range in the zoom. A 20% tightening can be a powerful thing to watch." The key is to move in and out as unobtrusively as possible. Don't call attention to a big moment by zooming in as fast as you can from a medium to a close-up shot.

A good reminder of how (and how often) to zoom is provided on television. Watch professionally shot interviews to see how infrequently and subtly the zoom is used.

SOUND

Although you're making a video memoir, clear sound is the most important technical requirement. Imagine your dismay if you end up with two hours of picture but not a word of your mother's wonderful anecdotes. At least if you have sound, the stories will be preserved.

A few pointers about sound:

- The built-in microphones on most camcorders are not great. They're getting better, but on the whole they don't provide the sound quality you should have for a memoir. "The further away your intended sound source, say a person speaking, the less the [built-in] microphone can pick up, and the greater the background noise," writes Peter Hitchcock in *Videography: The Guide to Making Videos.* The solution is to use an external mike, bearing in mind the same considerations discussed in the previous chapter on tape recorders. Lapel mikes for both the interviewer and the teller are preferable, but an external mike, properly situated, should also be fine.

- If you must use the built-in mike, do a thorough test to determine its range. The farther the camera from the teller, the less audible the sound.

- Most camcorders have a headphone jack. Wear headphones to test sound levels prior to recording and to monitor the sound during the taping.

- On outside shoots, wind and background sounds can interfere with the sound quality. Before recording, stop and listen to all the sounds your ear can pick up to determine if any would be distracting on the soundtrack. One obvious solution is to move to another location, perhaps a sheltered spot if wind noise is a problem.

- As stated previously, if the interviewee is soft-spoken, politely ask the person to speak a little louder than normal. Keep a sharp ear on the sound levels during the taping. If the voice level drops too low, you may have to stop and remind the speaker to increase volume or you may have to move the microphone closer.

LIGHTING

Bad lighting can ruin an otherwise wonderful interview, so be sure you pay attention to this critical detail. It's so disappointing to have an evocative story told by someone whose features are hidden in a dark shadow, as if the person's identity is being protected from public view.

Fortunately, most modern camcorders (circa 1990) work exceptionally well with ambient light, older models less so depending on the make. No matter the era of your camera, always test the lighting before starting a shoot. This is made much easier by using a color monitor.

A few pointers about lighting:

- You want the face, and particularly the eyes — "the windows of the soul" — to be well lit.

- Have the main light source, be it natural or artificial, shining on the subject's face. In most cases, you don't want the sole light source behind the subject (although sometimes a "back light" will help soften or remove shadows from too harsh a light in front). For example, be careful not to have the subject sit in front of a window through which bright sunlight is pouring, with the camera pointing at the window. If you do, the person's face will be almost impossible to see (the back of his or her head, however, will be basking in light!). Instead, have the subject sit facing the window, so the sunlight will fall on his or her face.

- For outside shoots, just as in photography, don't shoot into the sun. Have the camcorder operator's back to the sun, with the sun shining on the teller's face. It's often fine for the teller to be in the shade, as long as it's not too dark.

- If the natural light changes significantly, which it often does both indoors and out, you may have to adjust your lighting requirements. This could mean repositioning the camera and/or teller and/or adding artificial light.

- There are times, both indoors and out, when you need to use artificial lighting to boost the available light. This can be accomplished with anything from a standard light bulb (the wattage depends on the need) to a flood light used in photography. The most common mistake with this kind of lighting is to put it in a position that causes shadows to fall on the teller's face. One way of avoiding this is to "bounce" the light off a nearby surface, such as a wall or ceiling, rather than have it aimed directly at the teller's face.

Good lighting demands that you experiment beforehand. It almost always requires some fiddling and adjusting to get it right.

FRAMING AND COMPOSITION

"Framing refers to the borders of the shot," write the authors of *Producing a First-Class Video for Your Business.*" That is, what is inside them and what is left out. Composition refers to how elements are arranged within the borders. Part of the magic of [video] is its ability to show the viewer only what needs to be seen. This is the essence of framing."

Regarding composition, they write: "Alan Wurttzel, in the book *Television Production,* says 'Any shot which does not show the subject clearly or which unintentionally confuses the viewer is poor composition.'"

Some pointers on composition:

- The first and most basic step is to look, with a critical eye, at exactly what the camera "sees." This requires you to examine, in detail, everything that's within the "frame" of the picture, and how all the elements relate to each other.

- Try to find interesting and relevant backgrounds. You must look beyond where the person is sitting to perceive what else will be seen in the shot. Your goal is to have an attractive background that seems in keeping with the person and what the person is talking about. Rather than a bare wall behind the person, it's usually more visually stimulating if there are pictures, a book case, etc. If the teller is sitting in a single chair, a nice touch is to have a small table with flowers beside it, or a lamp.

- Move objects around to compose the shot. If there isn't an interesting background for your shot, create one yourself. Move tables and chairs, add plants, remove unwanted objects, etc.

- "One of the most common mistakes people make in composition," writes Peter Hitchcock, "is leaving too much space above the head. When that happens, the space above the head seems more important than your subject." Look in the frame to assess how much distance is left between the head and the top of the shot.

- Keep a lookout for how the color of the teller's clothes compares to the background. "For example, a person wearing a black suit, shot against a dark background," says Hitchcock, "would be hard to distinguish, so try a lighter background."

PROPS

As discussed previously, props can add a great deal to an interview. If you intend to have the teller read a letter, hold a photograph, show a medal, etc., make sure the prop is ready and within reach beforehand, perhaps on a table beside the teller. Instruct the camcorder operator to get a clear close-up of the prop as the teller speaks about it.

MAKEUP

A little makeup can help the teller look "warmer" (less pale) and prevent shining, especially if you're using lights. If the teller feels comfortable with makeup, encourage him or her to use it. (Many older men may not want it, although you can explain that everyone who appears on TV wears some makeup.) For men, either you or someone with you would likely have to apply it.

Mention to the women that bright lipstick and eye shadow usually don't look good on video. Subtle tones are better. What's needed is a light dusting of powder and some foundation to even out skin tones.

DRESS

My preference is that people look natural, so I suggest they choose clothes that are comfortable and representative of who they are. Having said that, here are some basic dress rules for video:

- Neutral colors work best, such as blue, yellow, green, etc. Extreme colors, especially red and black, don't reproduce on video very well.

- Avoid colors that contrast, such as black and white. Video technology doesn't cope well when it has to choose between two extreme colors. If you've seen a hockey referee's black and white striped shirt on television, you'll have noticed how the colors seem to shimmer and break up. This is called the *"moiré"* effect, and it also applies to any patterns with contrasting colors.

- Don't wear white or shiny materials. Because they reflect light, the iris of the camera has to adjust to tone down the brightness. The result is less light available for the teller's face.

DATE AND TIME

"Don't forget to use your camcorder's date and time generator (assuming your unit has one)," says Robert Wolenik in *Camcorder Survival Guide*. "In years to come it may be difficult to remember the chronological order of events. Date and time take the guess work out of it. You don't have to have it on the screen for long — just a few seconds is all that you really need."

TAPE SPEED

Most camcorders offer three tape speeds: SP (standard play, which records at the fastest rate); LP (long play, which is slower, and can record for twice as long as LP); and SLP or EP (slowest speed or extended play, which can record for three times as long as SP).

What's at stake with the different speeds? The faster you record, the better the picture quality. Use SP for a memoir. It's unlikely you'll need the extra recording time provided by LP and SLP anyway.

TAPE QUALITY AND CARE

As with audiotape, don't buy cheap stuff. Select high grade brand names.

Mandy Matson, in *Using Your Camcorder,* offers these tips about handling videotape:

- *"Use fresh tapes.* Don't recycle the ones you've been using to record programs. Each pass through a camcorder or VCR puts a little more wear on the tape, causing glitches (video static) and dropouts (momentary signal losses)."

- *"Keep your tapes away from magnetic fields.* They can erase what you've recorded." So don't have them near TVs, speakers or amplifiers and have them hand-inspected at airports.

- *"Keep your tapes clean."* That means in their boxes and away from dust and smoke.

- *"Keep your tapes warm and dry.* But not hot. Heat and humidity can do serious, irreversible damage. Videotapes don't like the cold much, either."

- *"Store your tapes vertically.* Over time, horizontal storage can damage your tapes."

- *"Don't store your tapes half-wound.* Leaving them like that can crease the tape."

11

A FEW WORDS ON EDITING

Less is more.

Robert Browning

If you want to produce a highly polished memoir, I recommend you learn at least the rudiments of editing audio or videotape. Editing is not a difficult skill to master, and requires only a little equipment and a bit of practice.

This chapter is intended as a brief introduction to the basic concepts of editing — as an inspiration to give it a try.

THE PURPOSE OF EDITING

You edit a memoir for three primary reasons: to take out unwanted material; to fit a maximum time for the final product; and to add elements, such as other interviews, still photographs, old home movies, etc.

The first reason — to remove material — can be for both creative intentions and time restrictions. Generally speaking, an edited interview is more interesting than an unedited one. That's because only exceptionally articulate and fascinating speakers say something fabulous each time they talk. It stands to reason that if you record several hours of conversation, there may be significant portions that won't hold an audience's attention as compellingly as others. "From four hours of videotaping you'll probably get an hour [of usable material] at the most," says Barry Broadfoot. Now that four-to-one ratio is for a highly professional end product, but the principle applies to amateur memoirs as well. By removing repetitions, long-winded preambles, meaningless digressions, dull or unclear anecdotes, etc., the edited version will likely be better than the original uncut conversation.

Second, you might edit to reduce a tape to a certain time limit. For example, you've taken it upon yourself to produce a video memoir of your grandparents to show at a family reunion. You've wisely decided the tape should run no longer than 60 minutes (a good maximum for a public viewing). But the interviews with your grandparents lasted several hours. Therefore, you must either edit the interviews or face an impossible — and unsolvable — mathematical problem: make several hours of raw content fit into a one hour production. I regretfully report that too many people, when placed in this predicament, scuttle their original plan to edit and just leave everything in. The result is a long and boring memoir rather than a "tight" and enthralling one.

The third reason for editing is to include elements other than the original interview. Instead of just one person — a "talking head" — your memoir could have interviews with several people, music, narration, special effects, titles, still photographs, etc. This documentary-style memoir involves more work and requires additional equipment and expertise. The finished product, however, is usually more interesting, layered, and wide-ranging than the single interview.

A BIG WORD OF CAUTION IS NEEDED AT THIS POINT. The original, unedited interviews are extremely valuable, despite their lulls and lapses. Don't discard them, tape over them, or destroy them in any way. Don't edit original audiotapes — make a copy of the original first (this doesn't apply to videotapes because you don't actually cut the tape during editing).

TAKING OUT

When asked, "How do you know what to take out?" editors will tell you their decisions are governed not by a rule book but by a sense of what constitutes interesting and essential conversation. Like a stage play, which treats the audience only to dialogue selected to advance the story and hold their attention, an edited interview should only contain material deemed interesting or necessary to the overall understanding of what's being spoken. In other words, it's a judgment call, and the more editing you do, the easier it becomes to make good judgments.

When faced with a long interview full of wonderful anecdotes that, for time restrictions, has to be reduced to a specified length, those judgment calls can seem impossible. "I can't take any of this out," is a cry I've heard in many an edit booth. Although I always sympathize with the editor's dilemma, my response is this: "The audience will never miss anything it doesn't hear." In others words, if you have absolutely no choice but to cut good material, you have to let go of your attachment to certain anecdotes and stories and take them out. You will miss them but the audience will never know they existed.

Be careful, however, not too become too zealous an editor and cut out too much. Your objective is to produce an edited interview that has a natural, unhurried feel. It's not good or necessary to eliminate every little pause or digression or mistake. In fact, it's better to leave those in so that the teller's speech characteristics remain evident.

To help give a sense of what to edit, compare the following examples:

- **Example 1**

Unedited version:

Q: What is your first memory?

A: I'm sorry, I didn't quite hear you. What did you say?

Q: I was wondering what your first memory was?

A: I'm not sure what you mean.

Q: Sorry, I guess I'm not being clear. Thinking back to when you were very young. If you search your memory to when you were a child, what is the first memory, the oldest memory you have. Maybe you were one or two or older.

A: Oh, I understand. Let me see now. I remember being three years old and my mother....

Edited version:

Q: What is your first memory?

A: Let me see now. I remember being three years old and my mother....

   •   **Example 2**

Unedited version:

Q: When did you first meet grandad?

A: When did I first meet him? That must have been in 1943 — almost 50 years ago — at a picnic. Now what picnic was that? You know, I can't remember it for the life of me. Maybe if I can remember who else was there it will come back to me. Oh isn't that awful (long pause). Was Elsie Blackburn there? She often held picnics out on the Blackburn ranch, which was quite a place. Her grandfather owned it and he was —

Q: That's okay not to remember. But you recall meeting grandad?

A: Yes. That I'll never forget. He had just graduated as a doctor and was all excited about going to Europe to help with the war. He had enlisted and was wearing his uniform, which made him look too handsome to resist!

Edited version:

Q: When did you first meet grandad?

A: When did I first meet him? That must have been in 1943 — almost 50 years ago — at a picnic. That I'll never forget. He had just graduated as a doctor and was all excited about going to Europe to help with the war. He had enlisted and was wearing his uniform, which made him look too handsome to resist!

INTERCUTTING INTERVIEWS

This process involves more than one interview, which you edit together — "intercut" — on one tape. For example, you interviewed three brothers, Jake, Pete and Hank, about growing up on the family farm in Saskatchewan in the 1930s. You asked each the same questions: Describe what you remember about the farm? How did you survive the Depression? What chores did you have to do? What was a typical day? What were your parents like? What animals were on the farm? What was the worst winter you remember?

The brothers gave similar answers to some questions, contradictory ones to others. Often they told the same familiar anecdote from different perspectives. Jake remembered some events that Pete and Hank had forgotten, and vice versa. By intercutting the three interviews you can weave an interesting "documentary" together. For example:

JAKE: A typical day started around six in the morning, with mother clanging a bell to get us all awake. She'd tried everything else to get us up but nothing worked so she got an old school house bell from somewhere. Boy did that snap you out of your sleep.

(Cut to Pete, who picks up the story.)

PETE: I remember one time I was so tired from haying that I even slept through the bell. Mother swears that she stood there clanging it right in my ear and I didn't budge. So she doused me with cold water and that still didn't get me up. I think she got my brothers to drag me out of bed.

(Cut to Hank, who picks up the story.)

110

HANK: Pete was definitely the worst for sleeping in. He says he didn't hear the bell but we know he did. What he's not telling you is that he was such a thickhead he could have it ringing in his ear without it bothering him. He'd rather have the ringing in his ear than get out of bed.

Notice how each speaker "advances the story." Although there's some repetition, what you have in effect is the same anecdote told by three different people, each with his own voice, mannerisms, etc.

When intercutting several voices, eliminate your questions as often as possible. Only leave a question in if it's necessary to understand an answer. For example, in the following exchange —

Q: What was the weather like that day?

A: Hot. Unbelievably hot.

The question is needed for the answer to make sense. But it's not needed in the next example:

Q: What was the weather like that day?

A: That day had the hottest weather I've ever experienced.

In the latter example, the answer stands alone and doesn't need the question for it to make sense. As a rule, let the tellers tell the story — if you can take out your question, by all means do so.

For a long memoir in which there is considerable intercutting, avoid an obvious pattern of speakers. For example, don't get into the rhythm of having Jake, Pete, and Hank always speaking in the same order. Let the story dictate who is speaking, which should result in an order that doesn't have any noticeable pattern.

EDITING AUDIOTAPE

You've all probably heard a sports report on radio that featured several edited comments:

RADIO ANNOUNCER: Last night the Toronto Maple Leafs captured their third Stanley Cup in a row, defeating the Anaheim Mighty Ducks 4 – 3. Here are some comments from the Leaf players:

FIRST LEAF: We all gave it 110%, what more can I say?

SECOND LEAF: What can I say. They were great opponents and we were fortunate to win.

THIRD LEAF: It's like, you put your pants on one leg at a time. Give it your best and, hey, what can I say?

All three comments were recorded separately but ran on the radio without any interruption. That's because the reporter took the three interviews and edited selected comments from them together into one seamless whole.

How was that done? The interviews were recorded on a cassette recorder after the game. The reporter returned to the radio station, dubbed (transferred) the recorded interviews from the cassette machine onto reel-to-reel quarter-inch audiotape. The reason that was done was to allow the reporter to edit or cut the tape.

Reel-to-reel tape is much wider than cassette tape, which makes it possible to edit on it. The material was dubbed at a speed of seven and one half inches per second. That means for every inch of reel-to-reel tape there is one second of recorded sound. Take out a ruler and measure seven and one half inches. That's a lot of tape for one second. Therefore, when you make an edit, there's a lot of room to work with — it's not like cutting a diamond where you have no leeway for imprecision.

If you're starting to get lost or confused, don't despair. Let me assure you that actually editing the tape is far easier than trying to explain (or read about) how to do it! The best way to learn is to watch someone and then try it yourself. Having said that, I'll continue nonetheless.

Basic editing

The basic edit is the removal of a segment of an interview. To do that you listen to the tape to determine what you want to take out. Next you locate the beginning of that segment and mark the spot on the tape with a grease pencil especially designed for editing. You then locate the end of the segment you want removed and mark it. Using a razor blade and an edit bar (easily purchased), you cut at both marks (thus removing the unwanted segment) and reattach the two ends of the tape with splicing tape. Sound easy? It is, once you get the hang of it.

How do you know where the words are on the tape? Reel-to-reel tape recorders have "recording heads." When the tape passes over the head, you hear what has been recorded. A few minutes experimenting on a tape machine will teach you how and where to locate the beginning and end of words.

Assembly editing

This process is the same as above except it involves assembling several interviews into one final package (like the sports example). Let's say you interviewed your mother and father at separate times and have an hour of tape with each of them. Your objective is to intercut the two interviews so the listener hears the two voices talking back and forth. To do that, you need to take material from each separate interview and edit it on to a third tape — the master tape — in an order decided by you. (When all the parts from the two separate tapes are assembled on the master tape, you can then edit the master tape for style and length.)

Equipment

You don't need much: a sturdy reel-to-reel tape machine that gives you access to the recording head area, which is where you mark your edits (pick one up at a garage sale); quarter-inch audiotape; dubbing cables; an edit bar; splicing tape; and grease pencils. All are available at basic electronics stores and, except for the tape machine, are relatively inexpensive.

EDITING VIDEOTAPE

The principles of editing video and audiotape are the same, so please consult **EDITING AUDIOTAPE** above before reading this section. The one major difference is that you don't actually cut videotape during the editing process. Instead, you either record over what you have already taped (in-camera editing); transfer segments (which have picture and sound) of your tapes to a master tape (assembly editing); or insert new scenes over an existing soundtrack (insert editing).

In-camera editing

Simply stated, in-camera editing is the process by which you record your material in the order you want it to appear in the final version. It requires detailed planning and disciplined execution.

For example, you intend to produce a memoir of your grandmother. You want to include some still photographs, interviews with her in different locations, her talking about her husband, etc. So you make the following plan:

- Begin with a close-up of a picture of her when she was a baby. Dissolve. Do the same for four other photographs. Fade out.

- Do five-minute interview about her early years. Fade out.

- Record her at piano singing song from childhood. Fade out.

- Do ten-minute interview about when she met grandfather. Fade out.

- Record her walking with grandfather in the garden. Fade out.

And so on. Because most camcorders have excellent pause buttons, fade and dissolve functions, and numerous other technical options (read your manual), you can produce what appears to be a smoothly edited tape without having to do anything beyond careful planning. By recording over segments that didn't work, you can correct mistakes or remove unwanted material as you go along.

Assembly editing

The concept is the same as for editing audiotape: material from various sources is assembled onto a master tape. To accomplish this you'll need a "source" or playback unit (either your camcorder or a VCR), which will play the unedited tapes, and a "record" machine (a VCR), into which you put the video equivalent of the master tape.

Because not all camcorders and VCRs are compatible, you may have to read your manual and/or talk with a dealer or expert to discover what cables, jacks, etc. are required to get them working together.

Peter Hitchcock, in his excellent book *Videography: The Guide to Making Videos*, outlines a nine-stage process for assembly editing with a camcorder as the "source" unit:

1. Ensure the VCR has flying erase heads...so that all edits are clean and glitch-free.

2. Connect the **output from the camcorder to the input** of the [record] VCR.

3. Select the shot you wish to transfer from the original tape playing in the camcorder.

4. Rewind the original tape a bit, and press **pause** at a point that allows you enough time to catch the exact selected image you want.

5. Prepare the VCR with a blank tape and place it in **line-in** mode, at VCR setting. Set the VCR to **pause in record mode.**

6. Put the camcorder in **play mode** and watch for your selected image to appear.

7. With your run-up time in mind [*most machines don't record right away. There is a second or so pause beforehand. By experimenting on your equipment, you'll determine your machine's particular run-up time.*], release the pause on the VCR to record.

8. Use a video monitor or television set to track what you are recording. At the point you wish to stop transferring from camcorder to VCR, press pause on the VCR.

9. Select the next shot you wish to transfer, and repeat steps 4 to 8.

Insert editing

Insert editing is a more advanced and complicated form of editing. For that reason I'm going to restrict my comments to a brief description. Most readers of this book are unlikely to employ it. If you are interested — and it's certainly worth learning — you will have to delve into it at a level beyond which I can describe in this section.

"Insert editing involves recording over undesirable shots with better, or more appropriate footage," writes Mandy Matson in *Using Your Camcorder*. "You see the results of insert editing on TV every day. A reporter interviews someone. She asks a question, he answers. But as he talks, we don't just see his face: we see the location, the reporter nodding her head, a close-up of the man's hands."

That's because pictures have been selected, timed, and inserted over the original soundtrack of the interview to create a connected and coherent final package. A memoir version would go something like this: during an interview with your grandfather, when he mentions the farm he grew up in, we see shots taken at the farm but continue to hear your grandfather's voice talking about the farm. Later on he mentions his war medals, and we see shots of the medals he's describing, etc.

Insert editing requires precise timing and planning, and a machine called an edit controller.

CUTAWAYS

You see these every day on television. A reporter is interviewing a politician and suddenly we see a shot of the reporter nodding, smiling, etc. This is a cutaway, and has been recorded to help in the editing process. Whenever you see a cutaway you can be sure what the speaker is saying has been edited.

If you plan on editing your video memoir, you might want to use cutaways. They can include shots of yourself; you "re-asking" certain questions; shots of the room or location of the interview; shots taken from behind the teller as he or she is talking, although the teller's actual words can't be seen; photographs; memorabilia mentioned in the interview; and so on.

To quickly learn about cutaways just watch the TV news.

SHOOTING STILL PHOTOGRAPHS

If you are shooting still photographs separately for editing into your video, the best way to do this is to lay the photographs on a flat surface such as the floor, mount the camera on a tripod, and use the macro setting to get a full-frame shot.

CONVERTING HOME MOVIES
AND SLIDES TO VIDEO

There are two basic methods: have a company do it for you (it's not very expensive; look under Video in the Yellow Pages for someone who does it in your area); or do it yourself. The latter option involves projecting the movies/slides onto a screen or white wall and videotaping them, or buying image transfer units that will allow you to transfer slides and negatives directly onto videotape.

TITLES

You see titles used on TV and in films every day. The most common is the brief appearance of a person's name and job description on the screen during a news interview. Just as familiar is the title and list of actors and production personnel appearing at the beginning of a film or TV show (the "credits"). Less common, although not unfamiliar, is the use of a title to indicate time or place — "Bogota, Colombia, 1962."

MUSIC

Music is wonderfully evocative and even the most sparing amount can create mood and atmosphere in your memoir. Be forewarned, however, that it is against the law to use music protected under copyright in any kind of public performance without receiving permission (which will cost you considerably, depending on who owns the copyright).

Whether playing your video to a group of relatives constitutes a public performance is up to lawyers to decide (technically it may be, although it's doubtful anyone would prosecute). If you charge or make any money or otherwise benefit through the playing of the memoir, the chances of litigation increase dramatically.

One solution is to purchase stock music from companies offering a library of music, but a fee is involved. Even easier is to perform or create your own music. If you have a tin ear, there's usually a musical whiz in the family or a friend who would be all to happy to get involved.

The best way to learn how to incorporate music is by listening to radio, TV, and film documentaries and to movie soundtracks. Note that the music is used sparingly; kept brief — only a small portion is usually used; timed to start and finish at a chosen moment; often "mixed" under a person's speaking voice at a low level so the listener doesn't have to choose between the music or the voice — the voice is much louder; and typically faded down and out as it departs.

The technical process for both audio and video music mixing requires planning, accurate timing, the monitoring of sound levels, practice runs, and the equipment necessary to facilitate a mix (more accessible for video these days than audio).

Caution: Don't record music directly onto an original tape unless you are absolutely sure you want it there permanently.

NARRATION

Narration involves the writing and recording of a script. It is typically used to introduce a production, create transitions from one segment to the next, explain necessary information in a tight and clear format, and conclude or sum up the production. It's by no means essential for a memoir but, as with music and other effects, it can add that extra professional dimension.

If you're considering narration, here are some suggestions:

- Study a documentary that employs narration to get a clear sense of how it's used.

- Keep it to a minimum.

- Although you can write the narration at any time, it's typically written last, for it's often used to help pull unconnected pieces together.

- Choose a good reader as your narrator.

- Practice beforehand.

For an audio memoir, you can always record the narration on a separate tape and edit it onto the master tape. A more professional approach is to mix it into the master tape, but that requires a studio or studio-type equipment.

For a video memoir, you need to time your narration to coincide with the visuals of your production. That requires you to do the following:

- Practice recording your narration as you watch the master tape to see when, where, and how long you should talk (and what visuals will be seen during your narration).

- Record your narration on a separate videotape as you watch the master tape on a monitor.

- Once you have an acceptable version of the narration, put the master tape in the record VCR and the narration tape in the source (camcorder or other VCR).

- Make an audio dub from the source to the VCR record tape.

A SOLUTION FOR THE NOT-SO-TECHNICALLY INCLINED

Many of the special effects such as music and narration may seem beyond your capability or require equipment you don't have. But, you'd like your memoir to benefit from as many of these extras as possible. So what can you do?

You can hire an audio or video studio to help you. For an hourly fee, you can get a professional technician to edit, add music, record, and mix narration, etc. in a studio. If you choose this route, here are a few pointers to help you get the product you want:

- Do as much planning and decision-making as possible before going to the studio. A lot of time (and therefore money) is wasted in studios because clients come without knowing what they want to do.

- Shop around to find what studios offer the best price. Don't be afraid to bargain — it's a seller's market these days.

- You'll probably get a lower hourly rate in off-hours, such as late at night.

- Some studios let you edit yourself, charging only for the facilities. Bring in a friend who knows how to edit, hire a broadcasting student (if your city has a community college offering courses in radio and television arts), or anyone else technically competent who will edit for free or a low rate.

12
VARIATIONS ON THE THEME

A New York socialite came into the salon of Walter Florell, mad milliner to movie stars and society, and announced she needed a hat at once for a cocktail party. Walter took a couple of yards of ribbon, twisted it around, put it on her head and said, "There is your hat, madam." The lady looked in the mirror and exclaimed, "It's wonderful."

"Twenty-five dollars," said Walter.

"But that's too much for a couple of yards of ribbon!"

Florell unwound the ribbon and handed it to her saying, "The ribbon, madam, is free."

American humorist Erskine Johnson

I never cease to be amazed at the boundless creativity and imagination of the so-called average person. It's my fervent conviction that anyone, if given the opportunity and encouragement, can produce works of art far beyond their perceived self-limitations.

The ever-expanding array of home recording equipment allows consumers to produce the kinds of videos and tape recordings that not long ago were the exclusive domain of a select few professionals. Now all you need is a small financial investment, a bit of effort, and whatever creativity you're willing and able to muster.

This book has explored some of the standard shapes and forms of a taped memoir. But there are endless other variations, and no rules, regulations, or restrictions to hinder what your imagination might compose. What follows is a brief list of alternative ways to use your camcorder or tape recorder to preserve family history. I know you'll come up with many others of your own.

THE NARRATED PHOTOGRAPH ALBUM

Your family photograph album probably contains faces both familiar and unknown to you. Videotape someone who knows who's who as he or she goes through the album and identifies everyone. This process will not only give you names and relationships ("That's Gertrude Montgomery. She was your mother's great aunt and the sister of...") but is sure to elicit anecdotes as well ("Gertrude was the black sheep of the family. She ran off with...").

You can either videotape the photographs as the teller narrates, shifting from shots of the teller to each pertinent photo; or you can shoot the photographs separately and edit them in afterward.

THE WALKING TOUR

Accompany the teller on a trip around old familiar places, such as the town where the teller grew up, a farm, favorite play areas, or anywhere that evokes memories of time and place. Ask the teller to describe what the buildings and surroundings were like in previous times, what memories are surfacing, how things have changed. This can be done for both video and audio.

THE HOUSE TOUR

If there's a special house or apartment in the family, or a room filled with pictures and memorabilia, have the teller guide you on a narrated tour. You can do the same for your own home, particularly if you're about to move. Go through each room, recording your descriptions, memories, and feelings as you go along. This is also a great opportunity to involve all members of your family, and it can be full of fun and spontaneity.

FAVORITE RECIPES

"Videotape [or tape record] your mother or grandmother cooking and explaining their recipes," suggests social worker Paula David. "There are so many recipes in our family that nobody has written down. My grandmother, for example, would break an egg and beat it into the batter and then fill the smaller piece of shell with sugar. I think it would be a great way to get them talking, of opening the memory."

INTERVIEW YOUR CHILDREN

Every year or so, sit down with your children and video or tape record them talking about themselves, what they do, their friends, etc. The content is entirely up to you but, like filmmaker David Grubin (see chapter 14), I would emphasize fun and lighthearted material, as opposed to the psychological probing made famous in the film *35 Up* (and its predecessors, *7 Up*, *14 Up*, *21 Up*, and *28 Up*). Part of the annual taping could be a measuring of the child's growth, display of artwork, school projects, sports equipment and trophies, etc.

EVERYONE IS AN INTERVIEWER

Don't become locked into thinking that only an adult between certain ages can do the interviews. Children can interview their parents and grandparents; grandparents can ask questions of each other; brothers can interview sisters. Experiment with different combinations that bring the generations together.

SCHOOL PROJECTS

Not all memoirs have to be made within your own family. A fascinating and valuable school project would be to have students plan and produce an oral history that focuses on their community. The possible themes of such an endeavor are endless and could encompass anything from a single event or individual to a large-scale history.

A FAMILY FEATURE MOVIE

Daphne Ballon of Atlantis Films suggests making a movie about the family. "You could write a script, give people lines, create a story with scenes," she says. "It would be fun even if people muffed lines and would get everyone involved."

TIME CAPSULE

Tape the members of your family saying something for a time capsule that you seal and leave unopened for a specified time. (I recommend at least 10 years, the more the better.) Perhaps give everyone five or ten minutes during which they could say, do, or show anything they wanted preserved in this historic document.

Make sure there is a well-kept record of where the capsule is kept and that it's stored in a dry and temperate location.

MEMOIR GROUP

Form a memoir group committed to producing video or audio memoirs. Just as there are countless writing groups in which the members encourage and criticize each other's work, your memoir group can do the same. This would be especially helpful for people who feel overwhelmed by the prospect of creating a memoir on their own or need assistance to cope with the technology.

Working within a group can have numerous benefits. Ann Silversides interviewed members of a seniors writing group in Uxbridge, Ontario for a documentary she prepared for CBC Radio's *Ideas* entitled "Senior Scribes." "Sights, smells, and feelings returned as members wrote," she says in her narration. "And around a table one person's anecdote would trigger another's memory."

REUNIONS

Organize a reunion and tape the proceedings. The reunion could be —

- A family or certain family members
- Close friends who have lived apart for some time
- School friends
- A sports team
- Musicians (your high school rock band, etc.)

TAPED DIARY

Record your experiences, thoughts, dreams, memories, etc. as you would in a diary.

13
LIFE STORIES

*Do you realize people will walk into an art gallery
and look at a painting on a wall in like a millimeter
of a second and judge it. But if they walk past a
monitor they'll give it two or three minutes.*

Lori Clermont, video artist

When I began researching this book, I placed a letter in several
newspapers asking people with any experiences making
audio and video memoirs to contact me. What follows are
excerpts from some of the responses, and from interviews and
other sources I came across while assembling material for this
book.

Morris Silbert, of Toronto, Ontario, has created more
than 40 memoirs of relatives, friends, and strangers. He uses
a tape recorder:

> I recently taped a cousin of mine, who had been
> taken prisoner-of-war at Tobruk during World
> War II. His brother was also taken prisoner there
> but they weren't together. They didn't know
> what had happened to each other. About two
> years went by and then my cousin was told he
> was being shipped out to Italy. They brought tall
> lorries — trucks — to ship the prisoners to the
> port. They were so tall that you needed help from
> the person on top to climb in. My cousin reached
> his hand up and the person who grabbed it and

pulled him up was his brother. Until that point he had no idea whether his brother was alive. It was a very exciting and wonderful story to preserve.

Now this cousin, who was from South Africa, knew very little about his family. His mother had died when he was two. After I had done the interview with him, he said, "You know, my sister died last month. I feel very bad about it. I know so little about my family." He didn't know I had interviewed his older sister during a trip to South Africa 13 years earlier. So I sat him down in the living room [and I played the tape] of his sister telling the story of his family. Well, I tell you, it was an emotional experience for him and all of us. And that shows you the value of preserving history.

Lori Clermont, of Halifax, Nova Scotia, uses video to help deal with some of the traumatic experiences of her youth. She was an inmate of St. Euphrasia's training school for girls in North York, Ontario run by the Sisters of the Good Shepherd in the late 1960s and early 1970s. In 1993 there was an ongoing police investigation of allegations that inmates suffered extreme physical and sexual abuse there. Clermont, who graduated from the Nova Scotia College of Art and Design in 1993 at age 37, has used video to help heal such violent memories such as the many times she spent in solitary confinement, "The Hole," at St. Euphrasia's:

When I started my work as a video artist, I thought it had to be political, it had to have a purpose, like functional pottery. I did a video called *Five Stories*. It was about my life. It was almost too real and it affected people and it made me realize how powerful stories are and how they can be used.

I'd never used a [video] camera before. I put myself in a ruin, in a building that was going to be torn down, where you could hear the water dripping down the walls. I had a red filter over the one-point lighting that I had. And I just started telling real stories about real situations. One in which I was locked up in solitary confinement for weeks on end. On the video I said [for example]: "The room is eight feet by eight feet square." I talked mechanically and non-emotionally. "With glossy green paint with a ten-foot high ceiling."

It was important for me, as part of my therapy, to listen to my stories. I think if people have undergone trauma, they might consider taping their stories from the beginning. At one point in their wellness they're going to wish they could go back.

Darrell Roberts, of Argyle, Nova Scotia sent me a collection of wonderful audiotapes he recorded of story poems he'd written about growing up in rural Nova Scotia. "I have impaired vision," Roberts says, "so I started making these tapes as a hobby. I figured the next generation might want to know how us old people lived." Roberts narrates the poems and stories as a raspy-voiced character he calls "grandpa." One tape begins with grandpa and grandma singing a duet, with piano accompaniment, of the song "Schooldays." Then "grandpa" begins to talk:

Hello there this is yer old friend grandpa comin' yer way once again. Yes sir, I'm goin' to try and make a tape here about little red school house days if I can. I don't know how I'll make out but I'm goin' to give it a try. I don't know why grandpa wants to make a tape about little red schoolhouse days because I tell ya, old grandpa, he never was a lover of the classroom. No siree.

There was lots of things that grandpa would sooner do than go to school. I'd rather be on the outside lookin' in than on the inside lookin' out. I guess I was sort of like a wild animal. I liked the wild life better, that is, travellin' the woods.

He then switches into verse, of which the following is a sample:

There were blackboards along both walls painted
    black
And written in chalk was "I see a cat."
Questions and fractions were written there too,
Which higher up grades had to figure and do.
Over the blackboards were maps which unfurled,
Where we learned about countries all over the
    world.
The old school house clock at the end of the room
Ticked off the time until recess and noon.
How often I've watched those hands slowly turn,
For life on the outside I always did yearn.

Our washrooms were located somewhere out
    behind,
Just two-hole affairs, real modern kind.
Separating the boys from the girls for defence,
Stood a high wide old barrier: a rough old board
    fence.
Yes sir, we used to look through the cracks of that
    fence,
Don't know what we expected to see,
But we looked anyway.

John Ainsworth, of Toronto, Ontario, is an avid movie fan and memorabilia collector. Although he has made home videos of his father and other family members since 1980, it was a video story connected to his obsession with actress Sharon Tate that I found most fascinating:

> After seeing [Sharon Tate] in *Valley of the Dolls* 12 times, I wrote her a fan letter. I got an autographed picture from her and from then on I watched out for her career. When she was murdered [by the Manson family] I wrote to the prosecutor and he replied saying that if I came to the trial he would get me a seat. This was in 1970. So on the first anniversary of her death, I went to L.A., visited her grave, and went to the trial. I was the only person not officially involved in the trial to get in. So the prosecutor told the media and I was interviewed outside the courtroom about why I was there and what did I think should be done with the killers. I rushed back to my hotel room to see myself on TV but it wasn't on. It was a 10-minute interview and I was so disappointed.

> A few weeks ago [in late 1992] I rented a video called *Great Crimes of the Century.* To my shock, I saw myself being interviewed as part of the segment on the Manson trial. There I was 22 years ago, at age 22. To see myself, hear how I sounded, brought back instant memories. It was just the most wonderful feeling to see the incredible innocence, the part of my life which was my youth, back again. It was also the most awful thing to realize that I'm not that way now.

Joyce Beaton is the author of *When Lightning Strikes,* a biography commissioned by the family of Evelyn Kennedy (1890-1985), which chronicles Evelyn's remarkable life in Canada. The title comes from the tragic coincidence that two of her children were killed by lighting 30 years apart. Beaton was greatly aided in her research by tapes that family members had made with Evelyn when she was 80:

> The tapes were most helpful although they were not well planned...and she was nervous. I don't think she was well coached on how to do this best. But the tapes provided information not forthcoming from the family. They didn't want to discuss anything controversial, but in the tapes she recalled incidents that I don't think the family would have told me. I find that interesting.

> She skirted around it a little bit but then she got enough to the point that her mother and father had split up, which in her time was just a shameful thing to do. With that knowledge, I took a tape recorder and went to the nursing home in the town she was raised in and found an old lady who had gone to school with Evelyn. She told me the rest of the story about the breakup. It turned out that Evelyn's father, who was a very well-respected doctor in town, had run around with not one but with several of his patients. The family wanted me to leave this out, but after a bit of a tussle they agreed to let me use it. [Leaving it in] makes her story more real.

Mary Makdator was interviewed for the book *Extraordinary Lives of Six Ordinary People,* an oral history project prepared in commemoration of International Day of the Elderly and Canada 125 by the Regional Geriatric Program of Metropolitan Toronto:

> I was born in old country [Ukraine] on June 17, 1906. We had nice house, a big house in Ukraine. We kept two rooms and rented three rooms after there was fire in city and people needed a place

to stay. You can't keep [for] yourself what you want. You have to share.

My mother had 14 children. She said she had to be in bed for two weeks after a baby. Sometimes they would live five or six weeks and die. Just five children lived. One day my baby brother started coughing. My daddy said to call the doctor because he was scared. He went 30 miles from home to buy medicine. The medicine was too strong. Strong enough for three men. I don't know what it was. It was [like] poison. The baby finished the medicine and died straight away. But he [the druggist] was gone and the police were looking for him. He ran to another country and never came back. Daddy nearly died too because he really wanted the baby boy.

Morley Torgov is a well-known novelist (*The Outside Chance of Maximilian Glick, A Good Place to Come From*). In 1979, he wrote the introduction to *From Our Lives: Memoirs, Life Stories, Episodes and Recollections,* a publication of writings produced by members of the Baycrest Terrace Memoirs Group. Although his comments refer to written memoirs, the message is relevant to anyone considering a memoir:

Fortunately these remembrances are not literary masterpieces. I say fortunately because, had the authors become absorbed with matters of form and style, the really important element — content — might have been sacrificed. As they stand, these pieces speak to us with simplicity, clarity, and honesty, and without any self-conscious attempts at art. Indeed, they evidence the achievement of higher art — the art of coming to terms with life, of "making the best of the worst," as one writer puts it.

14

THE FILMMAKER, THE JOURNALIST, AND THEIR PROFESSIONAL ADVICE: TWO INTERVIEWS ABOUT MAKING MEMOIRS

The ancestor of every action is a thought.

Ralph Waldo Emerson

David Grubin is a producer, director, writer, and cinematographer: the complete filmmaker. His films for television have won five Emmys. Among his many productions are the four-hour documentary films *LBJ* and *Healing and the Mind with Bill Moyers,* a five-part series for PBS.

PM: Have you ever recorded interviews with your own family?

DG: When my daughter was 5 — she's 23 now — before videotape was available, I had a camera and of course I had access to sync sound. Each year my sound man would come over and we would film an interview with her. I guess we did this until she was about 12 or 13, when she lost interest in doing them. When she was 21 I gave her this series of little interviews. You see her really growing up, and it's quite wonderful.

PM: A little like the film *28 Up.*

DG: Except I wasn't trying to do profound stuff. Really, the other extreme. I just wanted to have fun with her. I wasn't trying to do Piaget's psychology. I would ask her what she learned in school, things like that. I wasn't rigorous or anything in that we had to do them every birthday. I didn't want to have that feeling about it.

PM: How does your daughter feel about having the tape?

DG: I think she's really pleased. It's sort of a treasure to have.

PM: Most readers of my book will be recording an interview with an older relative. What do you think of the concept?

DG: I'd just like to say that it's a great idea but that people should have fun with [the making of memoirs]. That's a point I really want to get across. If you do it in the right spirit it can forge a closer relationship between the two of you. I was always interested in talking with my grandmother about her past. She came to this country when she was five. I always wanted her to dig up her old memories but she was determined to be an American and she pooh-poohed the past. She couldn't understand why I was so interested. I talked with her in person but I never did it on film. To have actually recorded it would have been quite wonderful and I think she would have liked it. And a grandmother to a child, I think, is probably easier, is probably less fraught with other kinds of tension than there might be there with a father or mother to a child.

PM: How would you go about filming it, compared to the biographies you've made?

DG: I'd say that the main difference between doing this and something like *LBJ* is that you want it to be fun, you want both of you to enjoy it, you only want something good to come out of it.

I would prepare for the interview. For the work I've done with famous people I learn everything I can about the person and the period, and I work out a whole series of questions. I have those available in a kind of chronology that makes sense to me. But when I do the interview

I let the thing free flow, like a river. So, I prepare a road map ahead of time and then veer off the road map, but I always know where I can come back on. I've found that's the way to get the most out of the interview.

My grandmother came from Austria-Hungary. To know that she came from somewhere near Auschwitz would raise a whole series of questions which she may or may not be able to answer. But if you didn't know that — if you hadn't done your research — it may never come out in the interview and you wouldn't be able to ask those questions.

PM: Learning about the period is so valuable.

DG: And often neglected. I mean, just to know what it was like when the first automobile came in, the first telephone. This can be fascinating and a lot of fun. But if you only think about the person's own story, a lot of good material can be missed.

PM: What do you say to interviewers who are concerned about asking personal questions?

DG: People are always relieved to talk, [that is,] real ordinary people, as opposed to politicians and diplomats who are trying to hide things as they talk. I've always found that when you show a real interest in people, and that they trust you're interested in who they really are and what they have to say, they'll tell you an awful lot about themselves. They do their best to tell you about themselves.

And often what they tell you may not be completely true but it's as true as they can make it. I guess they feel that in the end it's very rewarding to be able to talk about these things, even if they're quite personal. Maybe be able to talk about things they've never been able to talk about before with a relative. My anecdotes are sitting in my most recent film, *Healing and the Mind*. The last [segment] is "Wounded Healers" and that is a film of eight people sitting in a room doing group therapy, and in the afternoon doing individual therapy and in between they do yoga and art and all sorts of things. All of them have cancer. And in one way or another they're all trying to sum up their lives, trying to understand what it all meant. It doesn't mean they're all going to die but it means they're all aware of their mortality in ways you and I are not.

The only way the film would work, I told them, was if they could feel free to be themselves with the camera around. And very, very quickly people became happy that I was there. I remember one therapy session, we were late and they waited for us before they started. Because they trusted our presence, as if we were giving them some kind of reinforcement, as if our presence was saying, "What you have to say is valuable, and it's so valuable that we're here with a camera to record it, and we're going to put this on television. There's meaning in what you say."

PM: I don't know if it has a healing benefit, but I do think there's a benefit to be gained from the making of memoirs.

DG: I see obvious parallels with the memoirs. You're saying the same kind of message to people, about the value of their lives. And it can serve a healing purpose. When a father and son sit down and talk about something they may never had talked about before, that can be most powerful.

You know, you don't always have a chance to ask those kinds of personal questions [that can come up in a memoir]. You might ask "Why did you move to such and such a place when I was six years old?" And maybe the family has never discussed it before. For you, it was never explained and has always been a problem, because you didn't want to move. And then the father explains why — his point of view. Maybe it can clear up an old, sensitive problem that no one has talked about before. I think it's just wonderful for people [within families] to talk to each other like this. And if you look at it in that spirit, you'll forget about the camera and you'll just be talking and that in the end is the most precious thing — the talking — is more precious than the actual [taped] document. You know, you're inspiring me to do one with my father and mother.

PM: Memoirs deal with family myths. Can you talk about the value of exploring those myths.

DG: Every family has its myths, its stories. I believe that. Let me tell you about a film I made, *The Wyeths: A Father and His Family*. It's about N.C. Wyeth, who was one of America's greatest illustrators of children's books, and his five remarkable children. They include Andy Wyeth, the painter, two daughters who were also excellent painters, another daughter who was a music composer, and another son who was an inventor. He invented the plastic bottle that could hold carbonation.

Now in this biography, two stories emerge. There's the story the children want to tell, about a father who was a great loving, caring, enthusiastic man who produced these extraordinary, vital children. But at the same time there's another story that they can't help but tell. Of a father who was too big, who kept overwhelming them, that they can't get out from underneath because he's smothering them. It's a very good example of how the real story comes through along with the story people want to tell.

Andy Wyeth said that he'd always thought his brother Nat was the family clown until he saw the film and saw Nat talk about a tragic experience [Nat's four-year-old son was killed, along with N.C., when a car N.C. was driving stalled on a railway track. N.C. suffered a heart attack and the car was hit by an approaching train.] I think when you make a myth available to a family it helps them see what their place is in the family, and helps them examine the myth. It's not saying the myth is true, it's just helping in the understanding. New meanings and perceptions might come out of the process.

PM: So many people think their life is not worth talking about.

DG: They're so wrong. There's a great quote in the film by Nat Wyeth. He says, "The more I see of life the more I feel that writers are overpaid. My god, when you see what's out in front of you — your own life." All lives are extraordinary, and maybe a memoir can help people realize that what they do and think and say is important.

* * * * *

Natasha Stoynoff is a writer, photographer, and the Canadian correspondent for *People* magazine. In early 1993, she made a video memoir of her mother at her parents' home in Toronto.

PM: Why did you decide to do a video of your mother?

NS: She had a brain tumor and was getting worse, so I called one of her sisters in Los Angeles and told her to come right away and to bring her video camera.

PM: What did you hope to accomplish?

NS: She's the kind of person who says "I love you" in a way that no one else says it. I wanted to get her saying it to me on tape. But not just that. Ever since I was a 10 or 11, she and I would talk about how, when I had kids, she'd be a grandmother and we'd go shopping and have a lot of fun together. Now I didn't know if we'd ever be able to do that. But I want my kids, when I eventually have them, to know how sweet she is. I didn't think I'd ever be able to properly explain what she was like unless I had her on tape.

I have a million pictures of her and letters and cards, all sorts of things, but the only way to capture her personality was on film. You see, she has a quality, not to compare it to Marilyn Monroe, but she has a kind of angelic presence that takes up a room. You have to experience it in person. I felt that a video would capture that quality even better than the pictures did.

PM: How old was she when you did the video?

NS: She was 61, almost 62.

PM: How did you approach her to see if she wanted to do it?

NS: I didn't. I just went ahead.

PM: Did you anticipate she'd be in favor or apprehensive?

NS: Her condition had weakened her, so she wasn't really in a position to say yes or no. But my relationship with her is very positive and I knew she'd want me to do something like this. She trusts anything I do, and she has a very cooperative personality.

PM: Was she aware of the camera?

NS: For the first 20 minutes, yes. She'd be laughing and talking away but as soon as I got the camera up she'd stop. Then I got my aunt, who is a hair stylist in Beverly Hills, to cut my mother's hair. And that seemed to distract her and from then on it wasn't really a problem having the camera going. And I got this amazing kind of *cinema verité* thing. My aunt was cutting mom's hair, my father comes in and does his father shtick, my father and aunt start arguing, my brother shows up, and I'm going back and forth from person to person. It was like something out of "The Wonder Years" — real family dynamic in action.

PM: Did you ask your mother specific questions?

NS: I did, but again because of her condition they were different than what I would have if she'd been stronger. I said, "Mom, just say some nice things. Say happy birthday to your sister, say happy New Year." And she proceeded to say every greeting to everyone she could possibly remember, it was so sweet. Then I said, "Mom, throw me a kiss," and I zoomed in the camera, and she's saying, "Hi, sweetheart, I love you, I love you."

PM: What else did you do?

NS: I got my mom and her sister to sing all the Macedonian songs that they'd known since they were kids. She's a soprano and my aunt's an alto. My mother's speech and memory are affected by the tumor but when she sang the old Macedonian songs she remembered every word.

PM: Did you tell them what you wanted to do?

NS: Right. I turned the camera off, let them get their hair finished and put lipstick on, then sat them in the best light, especially for my mother. Then we began taping and all I had to do was prompt them every now and then with a song title. I got these really great sister scenes, them sitting next to each other, my aunt starting off a song and my mother joining in, and suddenly they would just hug and kiss each other and laugh. When that happened I'd zoom in and frame these two faces, these two beautiful blond European women who have so much love for each other.

PM: Did they become self-conscious?

NS: No. By this time they had accepted the camera. They'd become very playful.

PM: Were you concerned that what was happening was slow moving, not "good video," to use that phrase?

NS: While I was shooting, I did have in my mind that I was going to edit it, and exactly what I would take out. But about a week later, she caught pneumonia and went. into a coma, and my mom's other sisters from Boston and Arizona came. We watched the tape with some other relatives and everyone was saying, "Oh my god, this is so slow" and, at certain parts, "What did you shoot *that* for?" And I said, "Listen guys, when I was shooting this I just had me in mind, I was making the tape for me and my future kids." I felt almost like I was standing there nude in front of all of them because it was something very intimate for me they were watching. Especially the scene where I'm trying to get my mother to say "I love you," because I sound a bit desperate.

PM: Does that mean you're not going to cut it down?

NS: The journalist part of me thinks it's too slow. But the other part of me — the daughter of Maria — could never have enough of her on film, even if she was just sitting there staring out the window and all you could see was a thought that changed in her mind. So I don't care if it's boring to everyone else, it's not boring to me. I might produce an edited version for the relatives, a TV version you could call it, but I'll always keep a copy of the whole thing.

PM: A couple of technical questions. Did you use a tripod?

NS: No, hand-held. I like the way it moves around, isn't static.

PM: Lights?

NS: No, natural light, and it looks great.

PM: How do you value the tape?

NS: It's like a piece of gold or a precious jewel that I can put in my jewelry box and take out whenever I want to look at it. Knowing that I have it, no matter what happens, makes me feel calm, especially during this time of her illness. You see, I'm the kind of person who wants to keep things to show to somebody. I have a million scrapbooks, I keep copies of my favorite messages left on my telephone answering machine, I write notes to my daughter in my diary — I know I will have a daughter some day. One day, when she's 18 or 19 and something happens where I see that breakthrough happening from teenage rebellion to a greater understanding and appreciation of her family, I'll give it to her as a present. Wrap it up and say, "This is a tape of my mother, your grandmother."

PM: Are you going to make one of your dad?

NS: You know, it's funny but it never occurred to me to do that. He's on the tape a bit but the focus is almost entirely on my mother. I guess it's because he's not sick, but then he could go tomorrow. I guess that's what most people do, wait until someone is close to death before making the effort to do it.

PM: Most people never do it at all.

NS: That's true. I kick myself for not having rented a camera before. It costs so little compared to what you can create. But at least I know I have this time capsule, and if mom recovers, I'll be back to do a lot more. There are so many stories I want to hear her tell at least one more time.

15
CONCLUSION

The past is but the beginning of a beginning.

H.G. Wells

How often have you heard someone lament, following the death of a parent or other loved one, that it was now too late to express true feelings, ask certain questions or attempt to resolve old problems? Perhaps you have experienced this yourself.

One of the truly perplexing human traits is our fear of speaking truthfully and intimately with those we are closest to. We seem more able and willing to divulge our innermost thoughts to strangers in bars and airplanes, radio talk show hosts and paid therapists. Interestingly, the vast majority of people I interviewed for this book, both formally and informally, volunteered that it might be too difficult to do a memoir with a parent. Grandparents were deemed ideal subjects as it was far less likely any raw emotions or frictions would arise during a taping.

Although by no means am I suggesting all people share a reluctance (fear is a more apt word in many cases) to speak directly with their parents, I think more than enough feel this way to make it well worth noting. This is a sad reflection of how difficult it can be to communicate intimately within the family unit where, in theory at least, it should be the easiest.

Another unfortunate human characteristic is the tendency to denigrate ordinary lives (i.e., lacking in celebrity) as unimportant and without merit. Since dabbling in the world of memoirs, I've repeatedly heard people beg off being profiled by claiming: "I'm not famous. I haven't accomplished anything worth talking about."

Nothing is further from the truth. "I don't think there is any such thing as an ordinary mortal," Joseph Campbell, a foremost authority on mythology, told interviewer Bill Moyers in *The Power of Myth*. "Everybody has his own possibility of rapture in the experience of life. All he has to do is recognize and then cultivate it and get going with it. I always feel uncomfortable when people speak about ordinary mortals because I've never met an ordinary man, woman, or child."

All lives are rich and overflowing with experiences, observations, and feelings worth recording. By making a family memoir, you are saying that — and more — to everyone involved, including yourself. You are also taking the opportunity, and perhaps the chance, to sit down and talk intimately with someone you care about, whether there's friction between you or not.

I can't make any promises about what a family memoir will accomplish — it's going to be unique for everyone. But I am willing to predict that you will not regret having done it, and that future generations will thank you.

One last word of advice — make sure you make copies of your tapes, and keep them in a different location from your home (just in case of fire, flood, or some other disaster).

Good luck and have fun!

ANOTHER TITLE IN THE SELF-COUNSEL SERIES BY PAUL McLAUGHLIN

HOW TO INTERVIEW
The Art of the Media Interview
Paul McLaughlin

Professional interviewers — on radio, TV, and in print — make interviewing look so easy. How do they do it? Does being a good interviewer depend on having the "right" personality? Or is it simply a matter of learning a set of techniques that guarantee success every time?

Author Paul McLaughlin draws on the experience of the professionals to examine the art of effective listening, the importance of research, pointers on obtaining interviews, how to prepare questions, and the specialized requirements of print and broadcast interviews. A highlight of each chapter is the feature interview with well-known interviewers such as Patrick Watson, George Plimpton, and Barbara Frum. $9.95

Some of the topics explored in this book are:

- where to track down research material

- how to line up interviews

- how to use other sources to develop a profile of the interviewee

- why you shouldn't be afraid of silence

- how tone of voice can affect your interview

- the best locations to choose for your interview

ORDER FORM

All prices are subject to change without notice. Books are available in book, department, and stationery stores. If you cannot buy the book through a store, please use this order form. (Please print)

Name _____

Address _____

_____

Charge to: ❑Visa   ❑ MasterCard

Account Number _____

Validation Date _____

Expiry Date _____

Signature _____

❑Check here for a free catalogue.

IN CANADA
Please send your order to the nearest location:
Self-Counsel Press
1481 Charlotte Road
North Vancouver, B. C.
V7J 1H1
Self-Counsel Press
8-2283 Argentia Road
Mississauga, Ontario
L5N 5Z2
IN THE U.S.A.
Please send your order to:
Self-Counsel Press Inc.
1704 N. State Street
Bellingham, WA 98225

YES, please send me:

_____copies of **How to Interview,** $9.95

_____copies of **Producing a First-Class Video
                    For Your Business,** $14.95

_____copies of **A Family Remembers,** $11.95

Please add $2.50 for postage & handling.
Canadian residents, please add 7% GST to your order.
WA residents, please add 7.8% sales tax.